EVERYONE ... ign aid — machinery rus ... aders lining their pockets, ... ureaucratic snafus.

But a chilling, almost unbelievable story remains untold, one which shows an underside to foreign aid that is far more damning than the long and sorry list of failed but well intentioned attempts to relieve human suffering.

Not only can foreign aid dismally fail to help, all too often it becomes an instrument of harm that plunders the environment, increases human suffering, and even violates the human rights of those whom we, here at home, think we are helping.

At first glance, the villains in this piece are the huge energy projects, especially the hydro dams, that flood thousands of people off their land to uncertain and usually unhappy fates, in the process robbing them of their livelihood, destroying their culture, and trampling on their religious rights.

But the perpetrators are not the individuals that okay these devastating projects but the process that permits these atrocities to occur — a process that is tainted at every step of the way, from the role of our own governments to that of the governments in the Third World.

In clear, uncompromising language, *In The Name of Progress* spells out the damage that our foreign aid has wrought, explains where the process went wrong, and then prescribes the remedies needed to prevent foreign aid from doing more of the same in future.

**PATRICIA ADAMS** is a former advisor to the World Council of Churches' Energy Program and a Director of the Environment Liaison Center in Nairobi, Kenya.

**LAWRENCE SOLOMON** is an international lecturer and former advisor to President Carter's Commission on the Global Environment and is the author of numerous books.

THE AUTHORS live in Toronto, Canada, and work for Energy Probe, the internationally acclaimed research group.

## Also from Energy Probe Research Foundation

***Energy Probe***

*Power At What Cost* (by Lawrence Solomon)
*The Conserver Solution* (by Lawrence Solomon)
*Energy Shock* (by Lawrence Solomon)
*Over A Barrel* (by Jan Marmorek)
*Radiation Alert* (by David Poch)
*Zero Energy Growth* (by David Brooks)

***Probe International***

*Damming The Three Gorges: What Dam-Builders Don't Want You To Know* (Edited by Gráinne Ryder)
*Environment Held Hostage: How Debt Is Affecting The Third World (by Patricia Adams)*

***This edition made possible through grants from the Charles Stewart Mott Foundation and the Margaret Laurence Fund for Peace and the Environment.***

# IN THE NAME OF PROGRESS

## The Underside of Foreign Aid

*Patricia Adams and Lawrence Solomon*
***A Probe International Project***

Earthscan Publications Limited
London

This book is dedicated to
Joan, and to Mary

First published 1985 by Doubleday/Energy Probe



This edition published 1991 by
Earthscan Publications Ltd
3 Endsleigh Street, London WC1H 0DD



British Library Cataloguing in Publication Data
Adams, Patricia
In the name of progress: the underside of foreign aid
I. Title II. Solomon, Lawrence
338.91

ISBN 1-85383-121-2

Cover design by David King

Earthscan Publications Ltd is an editorially independent subsidiary of the International Institute for Environment and Development (IIED; charity number 800066).

Printed and bound in Great Britain by
The Guernsey Press Co. Ltd, Guernsey, Channel Islands.

# Contents

# IN THE NAME OF PROGRESS

# Foreword

## *"Unto the Third and Fourth Generation"*

THIS BOOK IS AUTHORED by courageous spirits. It challenges commonly held myths about energy and progress in today's world. It poses questions about collective presuppositions and assumptions we hold about foreign aid, population, resources, and the needs of the Third World. It slaughters sacred cows. It punctures inflated myths. It proposes alternate ways for the future. But more importantly, it raises the question of what it means to be fully human in a technological, industrial age.

I found one of the exciting assumptions underpinning the book to be the understanding that ecology and care of the earth and its resources is a collective human right. That collective human right to a future, which is as old as the Bible's *unto the third and fourth generation*, is as fundamental and basic as the personal and individual rights also enshrined in the *International Bill of Human Rights.*

What we need to recover is a bold renewed vision of the calling of humans to be partners to each other, and gardeners of the earth. Nothing short of the partner/gardener combination will do. Both require the basic orientation of humankind to be that of caring, a quality which requires a continuous relation to the future. To the extent that we care responsibly for each other, and for the earth and its resources, we are fully human.

To think in these terms is to plummet us into the center of the spiritual struggle of the 20th century — the struggle to find a future where we do not abdicate responsibility, command pretentious mastery or massive plundering of the earth. Rather, in this future we are invited to care together for the earth, its peoples and life-forms in just, responsible and merciful ways.

It is not reassuring reading, calculated to make us feel more at ease with ourselves or with our assumptions and practices. Yet it is full of hope because it looks to alternatives in the present and the future. I commend it to your reflection.

Lois Wilson
President, World Council of Churches

# Foreword

## *Foreword to the 1991 Edition*

WHEN WE FIRST BEGAN to investigate the workings of the international aid agencies in the early 1980s, few members of the public had heard of the World Bank or its sister multilateral development banks, and of those that had fewer still had any inkling that they might be contributing to the Third World's plight. The press, likewise, was in almost total ignorance. ("How does the World Bank work?" one producer at the Canadian Broadcasting Corporation asked us. "Can I open an account there?") So too were most politicians and bureaucrats not directly involved with the aid establishment. The environmental groups we worked with on other matters were similarly preoccupied with their own priorities.

Though we didn't know it, the isolation we felt in Canada was being experienced in other countries, by colleagues as yet unknown to us. Citizen groups in Third World countries were just starting to realize that their problems – which were increasing in magnitude – lay not just with the ambitious plans of their national leaders but also with Western lenders that were enabling those leaders' plans to proceed. Organizations concerned with the rights of indigenous peoples – often staffed by anthropologists who had spent years working with besieged tribal communities – began to recognize that the Third World community they were championing was but one of many under siege, and that the siege was laid by a curious type of progress, one marked by corruption, illegal expropriation of lands, and other perverse forces antithetical to their well-being. A scattering of environmental groups from the developed world – in Europe, in the U.S., in Japan and Australia – had, like us, begun to track down the financiers of this global destruction, and to assemble an understanding of their methods.

It didn't take long for these groups to lose their sense of isolation. With increasing frequency, meetings among them began to occur all over the globe, and while the meetings often focussed on different issues, they all had a common thread – the destructive role of the World Bank and its sister international aid agencies. In 1984, groups fighting the damming of the world's river valleys found each other at a conference sponsored by the Environmental Policy Institute of Washington; and in 1987 in Malaysia, at a conference sponsored by the Consumers Association of Penang, groups fighting the destruction of rainforests found each other and formed the World Rainforest Movement.

The result of these meetings, and the consequent ability to compare notes, to learn from one another's experiences and methods, and to draw upon one another's staff, materials, and other resources was explosive: literally thousands of citizen groups from most countries of the world are now joined in a variety of networks and coalitions, swapping information about development bank activities and working together on campaigns to reform them. The World Bank and its sister development banks are no longer anonymous organizations, free to carry out their activities unnoticed by all but those directly affected. They have become organizations under increasing scrutiny, being watched and called to account by congressional bodies and citizen groups alike. The World Bank is increasingly identified as an agent of undesirable change. In India, 60,000 people demonstrated against local officials and the World Bank in 1989 at the site of the Sardar Sarovar dam project, which threatens to flood 90,000 people off their land. The protest was the largest against a development project the sub-continent had ever seen.

In response to this pressure, the multilateral banks began to acknowledge their culpability. The first *mea culpa* came in 1987, when World Bank President Barber Conable admitted that the Bank had been "part of the problem in the past" and promised sweeping changes. The Bank's environmental staff soon increased tenfold, with some 60 new positions created, followed by a green tide of issue papers, action plans, and other measures designed to protect the world's environment. The Inter-American Development Bank followed suit and reversed its opposition to creating an environmental department, giving in to the long-held demands of many environmentalists.

By 1989, the World Bank's president reported that one-third of Bank projects had "significant environmental components" designed to mitigate environmental damage. As the Bank reasoned in an environmental report to the Bank/IMF Development Committee, "If the project is potentially very damaging to the environment, and if Bank participation could do much to reduce the damage but would not eliminate it entirely, the net gains from participation must be the deciding factor."

But closer scrutiny of those projects revealed many environmental disasters in the making, with the Bank's "environmental components" amounting to window dressing: the same destructive projects as before could be funded, the *New York Times* reported, but they might now be adorned with a row of trees around the project perimeter. In fact, the rationale in the World Bank's environmental report was not new – it has been repeatedly used over the years to justify reckless lending. In the opinion of one U.S. Treasury official: "There is no project too destructive, and too costly, that the World Bank will not throw hundreds of millions of dollars at to try to make it better. In fact, the worse the project, the more urgent the justification for the bank's involvement." Without the Bank's involvement, however, these environmentally destructive projects would rarely proceed at all, removing any need to make them less distasteful.

Beneath the Bank's environmental facade, it can't help doing what it was designed to do: move large amounts of money to the Third World. The requirement to scrutinize the environmental implications of its lending can only slow down the movement of money, making the additional environmental staff, and environmental budget, an irritant. Bank staff advance their careers by building up large loan portfolios and keeping them moving, not by slowing down the project pipeline to ensure environmental and social quality. Little wonder, then, that the environmental staff is kept away from the mainstream of decision-making, or that in 1989 only five of the Bank's 45 structural adjustment loans – large loans tied to economic reforms instead of to projects – explicitly addressed environmental concerns.

Reform at the World Bank has proven illusory; meanwhile, the Bank's destructive ability has been magnified by a $75 billion increase in its capital, which will allow it to nearly double its lending capacity. The only way to move more mountains of money will be through building more roads, hydro dams, and other large capital-intensive infrastructure projects, especially if the Bank follows through on its plan to reduce its structural adjustment lending.

AS THE FIRST EDITION of this book went to press in late 1984, the world learned to its horror that thousands and perhaps millions of Ethiopians were starving to death. The largest aid relief effort in history ensued, as people around the globe opened their hearts and their pocketbooks to help save the African nation from its dual disasters of drought and famine. Though too late for our first edition, we nevertheless decided to investigate the roots of the famine, and discovered that the world was helping to rescue victims of earlier aid efforts.

In the 1960s, the United Nations Food and Agriculture Organization proposed converting large tracts of central Ethiopia's Awash River Valley to sugar cane, cotton, and banana plantations. The project called for a series of dams on the river to provide both water for the crops and electric power for the capital city, Addis Ababa. Because the plan was so ambitious, the World Bank and the African Development Bank were brought in to help finance it.

Before the construction of the dams, the valley's rich floodplains – a mixture of savannas, swamps, and riparian forests nurtured by the semiannual floods of the Awash river – had supported 150,000 people. But with the damming of the river, flooding decreased dramatically. As the valley's bottomlands became arid, the land could no longer support its inhabitants. To the Afar, one of several tribes in the region, the misery wrought by the dams was so severe, so much worse than the droughts and the other hardships of the past, that it was explained as a punishment from God.

To make way for the plantations, lands traditionally held by the 20,000 people were expropriated, mostly without compensation. Forced to leave, the people and their livestock crowded onto lands near the newly irrigated plantations. One by one, the displaced tribes began to spill onto the lands of their neighbors. Normal migration routes were blocked, and tribal warfare intensified as the region's land base eroded. When the rains failed in the early 1970s and again in the early 1980s, the people, bereft of their former resources, became wards of famine relief stations.

Until a few years ago, a Third World community faced with the flooding of its farmland by a state hydroelectric project or the removal of its forests for pulp production was all but helpless. Generally it was given no say in the decision, let alone compensation for the loss of its property, and Westerners would learn of the project too late to intervene, even though the project was typically built by Western engineers using Western tax dollars.

Today, that community is as likely as not to have a fax machine or to be able to reach local environmentalists who – via fax, phone, or electronic mail – can reach a global network of environmental, human rights, and native rights activists. Within days, the project's developers can be identified, environmentalists in the donor country can be enlisted, and an international campaign mounted. Though most projects nevertheless proceed to completion, through this process literally dozens of ill-conceived projects are being stopped, and many more slowed or improved. As the ease of communication rises and as information flows improve, the rejection rate for bad projects can only increase.

The World Bank and the other multilateral institutions may not be any closer to real reform today than when this book was first published – if anything, they may be closer to obsolescence as those advocating reform begin to ponder whether their efforts might be better directed at closing the Bank down. The Bank has analyzed its environmental problem as a public relations problem, and has become expert at green rhetoric, lulling donor countries into thinking that it is benefiting the environment while carrying out business as usual.

But whatever happens to the Bank, thanks to better communication among groups around the world, the lot of the Third World's poor and the environment upon which they depend is looking up. The contagion of democracy sweeping the globe has yet to reach every corner of Eastern Europe, of Asia, or of Latin America – but where it has taken hold the people have begun to be empowered, and with empowerment comes protection of their environment and of their right to make the choices that affect their lives.

# Preface

## *The Myth Makers*

"…. nuclear energy is a natural force offering immense present and potential benefits to mankind, we would be unethical not to be promoting its use. Furthermore …. those opposing nuclear energy must accept ethical responsibility for causing deaths, human suffering, and environmental damage." — J.A.L. (Archie) Robertson of Atomic Energy of Canada Limited, in a brief submitted to the Interfaith Hearings on Nuclear Issues, September 24, 1984.

NO ONE WANTS to feel that he is living at the expense of others or that he is advocating policies that discriminate against others, especially when those others are the poor in the Third World.

Yet that is what Energy Probe found itself accused of in the late 1970s by advocates of nuclear power who were arguing that it was immoral of us to want to deny either the West or the Third World this technology.

On the face of it, there seemed to be merit to their arguments. The world's store of non-renewable resources was diminishing, and it was diminishing largely to feed the appetites of the affluent countries of the world: a switch by the West to nuclear power promised to conserve fuel for the Third World. And what if the Third World did need nuclear technology to develop its industries? How could the West consign it to technological backwardness and a low standard of living if nuclear power was the only energy source that could eventually meet the needs of its massive population?

We began to investigate the effect on the Third World of the policies that we were advocating at home and that took us beyond the nuclear issue and beyond our own borders. Our information came from international agencies like the United Nations and the World Bank, from the national agencies of Western countries and Third World countries, and from our counterparts in the Third World — other citizens' groups like Energy Probe.

The information from the national and international agencies was consistent with all that we had heard about the Third World's problems. The energy situation was desperate: oil bills were bankrupting countries and the forests that provide fuelwood — the main energy source for the Third World's poor — were being cut down at an alarming rate. The world's deserts were inching forward relentlessly, and massive infusions of Western aid were essential if the fuelwood crisis in these poverty-stricken areas was to be alleviated.

But the information from the citizens' groups in these

countries clashed with much of what we had heard, not so much about the nature of the energy crisis, but about its causes. Where governments and official agencies point the finger at the peasants who chop down their forests for fuelwood, the citizens' groups point the finger at state and multinational logging companies, and at the foreign aid agencies that fund them, for leaving the peasants so little to live on that they have no choice but to overcut their own forests; where the agencies point to the benefits of major development projects such as hydroelectric dams and fast-growing tree plantations, the citizens' groups point out that these projects have hurt those who need help the most, ultimately setting development in their countries a step backward rather than forward. We soon came to realize that the groups' explanations of the origin of their woes — which came to us from different cultures, countries, and continents — formed a consistent argument at odds with those of the official agencies.

All these revelations, but particularly those about the underside of foreign aid, clashed uncomfortably with our sensibilities. Foreign aid projects, we had grown up to believe, were supposed to help the lot of the poor, but case after case involved the poor fighting these projects, especially the hydroelectric projects which flood vast numbers off their land.

We wrote letters to senior officials in the Canadian government, which was helping to fund several dams that were being fought, to see if we could confirm the very serious charges that had been made. In other letters we also asked for examples of hydroelectric projects which had been successful in helping the Third World's poor, in order to balance the overwhelmingly negative information we had been receiving.

The President of the Canadian International Development Agency and others replied, but to our dismay the officials denied responsibility for some projects because Canada's funding had been indirect, through multinational aid consortiums like the World Bank. The officials likewise denied responsibility for another project — even though a CIDA press release had trumpeted Canada's financing — because Canada had not been the sole funder. And instead of answering our questions about specific projects, the officials evaded some, answered others incompletely, and would speak only theoretically and in generalities about the overall benefits of hydroelectric aid projects.[1]

It became clear to us that the government officials were unable to refute the claims of the citizens' groups. More surprisingly, the government, despite repeated requests, had failed to provide us with details of a single example of a model hydroelectric project.

No doubt such projects exist, but because the responsibility of our foreign aid officials generally ends with the disbursement of funds, because they do not need to live with the consequences of their projects, they do not need to know, and so do not know, of their effect on the region. The people in the regions to be flooded do not have the same sense of detachment: they are intimately aware of what the projects will mean for them because they intimately understand the environment they live in.

The groups in the Third World that these citizens have formed have a remedy for their woes, the same kind of remedy that citizens' groups in the West advocate for their own countries — opening up the development process to the public to give everyone affected a stronger voice.

The big difference between the citizenry here and there

is that people in the West generally have more power. We have access to the press when our industry or government spokesmen present untenable plans based on unsupportable statements, such as the claim that nuclear power will be too cheap to meter or the assertion that promoting energy conservation is tantamount to advocating a return to the caves. Ultimately, we have a vote at the ballot box if the issue becomes prominent enough.

In the Third World there is often no ballot, and the press is often controlled. Because the multinational corporations, international aid agencies, and agencies of our own governments that operate in Third World countries do so in secrecy,[2] the people in the Third World find it all but insurmountable to counter official plans, which can so profoundly affect their lives.

In this respect, Third World citizens are not alone. Citizens in the West also have difficulty obtaining information to counter these plans: all that we generally hear of the foreign activities of these institutions, which nominally act on our behalf, is what they, their consultants, and the Third World governments — all having vested interests — want us to hear.

Because most people in the Third World are voiceless, and because those with a vested interest have a near monopoly on information that comes from the Third World, our society has grown up with a distorted view of life in Third World countries. We don't all believe all the myths described in this book, but most of us believe most of them and know people who believe the rest. Consciously and subconsciously, these myths dominate our perception of how the Third World works, and until there is an unfettered flow of unfiltered information between the people of the rich and poor countries, the existing myths will remain and new myths will be created.

Patricia Adams
Lawrence Solomon

# Introduction

## *In the Name of Progress*

"Is the meaning of 'progress' for native peoples inevitably genocide?"
— Question posed by two dozen indigenous people from countries around the world at a Washington, D.C. Conference, Oct. 12, 1982.

BECAUSE WESTERN GOVERNMENTS are more or less representative of their citizens, and because gross abuses of state power — such as persecution of minority groups or the invocation of martial law — are rare occurrences in the

West, we tend to equate a country's policies with its people. When a government representative of West Germany, or France, or Japan is quoted in the press, we assume he is speaking with the weight of public opinion behind him and, for good reason, do not ordinarily bother to distinguish between the views of the government of the country and those of its citizens.

We extend this logic to undemocratic regimes at our peril. When a government is as unrepresentative of its people as is the case in much of the Third World, or when a charismatic leader acquires power over a country's legislature and other institutions, as occurred in the Philippines under Ferdinand Marcos, and in Tanzania under Julius Nyerere, what furthers the plans of the national government may bear no fruit, or a bitter fruit, for its people.

When President Marcos came to power in 1965, the Philippines had one of the fastest growing economies in South-East Asia. It now has the only severely contracting economy in the region, 50 percent inflation, and the second-largest foreign debt in the continent. According to a study by the University of the Philippines, the country's economic reversal can be traced to the concentration of government power that allowed privileged individuals and groups to use the government to promote their private interests through a variety of instruments, including government guarantees for their foreign loans. The government itself embarked on ambitious projects to bring about the economic future Marcos wanted, building grandiose roads, bridges, and dams without concern for the economic future that the common people were independently pursuing.[1]

President Nyerere had a different ambition for Tanzania's economy, but it was not his people's ambition, despite his personal popularity with them: to create his "socialist villages" required forced collectivization and wholesale relocation of 15 percent of Tanzania's population.[2] As with Marcos's plans, the citizenry who were expected to carry out Nyerere's plans could not fully trust, or understand, the role his government had in mind for them. Because the populace played no part in formulating the state's plans, and in shaping them to personal goals, the national plans for the national economy collapsed.

In the remote rural areas of Tanzania, the good times can come when the national economy is depressed, the national debt is growing, international commodity prices are low, and foreign exchange is unavailable. It is then that transport vehicles cannot be repaired for lack of spare parts, roads cannot be repaired for lack of material, and the support services believed to be crucial to agricultural development stop. The people in the villages can neither get their food to market nor want to because prices are too low. "When villagers cannot get their produce to market, it stays in the villages – they eat it themselves," explains Urban Jonsson, the United Nation's Children's Fund representative in Tanzania.[3] Standing conventional theories of national economic development on their head, Jonsson explains "their families eat better because of the national economic crisis. We must distinguish therefore between the state economy, which is in extreme crisis, and the village economies, many of which are doing quite well – and over 80 percent of the people in Tanzania live in the villages."

Another effect of the national crisis which has become apparent in some parts of Tanzania is a switch from cash crops like coffee beans, which are of little use in the village, to crops like maize, which means more food for families. According to the editor of *International Agricultural Devel-*

*opment*, local self-sufficiency improves when national policies go awry.[4]

The national policies themselves, though often conceived in the Third World, could not be brought to term without the backing of Western financial institutions – foreign aid agencies the most prominent among them[5] – which have spent billions building elaborate transportation systems, communications systems, and other infrastructures which they consider necessary building blocks of a successful economy. But these imported systems persistently break down because the skills required to maintain and renew them cannot be as easily imported, and the motivation to learn them cannot be manufactured. Since the demand for these systems did not come from the people but from their rulers, who had a vision of how the ruled should be organized, the billions lent by the international financial institutions have done little but feed the dreams of a ruling elite.

These "have-money-must-lend" institutions, as they are called by Manuel Ayau, the President of Universidad Francisco Marroquin in Guatemala, have been "one of the main causes of the sad state of economic affairs in Latin America." Because they are in league with spendthrift politicians, "a continent rich in natural and human resources is now regressing to a standard of living of pre-debt days, having mortgaged its own – and its children's – future."[6]

International financing that is given to unrepresentative governments may harm more than the national economy; it may harm large numbers of people, particularly when targetted to major capital projects, because large projects invariably affect the environment and those who directly depend on the environment.

In the last three decades, no capital projects have received more funding, or caused more grief, than energy projects.[7] Most prominent among them are hydroelectric dams, which generally flood large numbers of rural people off their land to uncertain, and usually unhappy, fates. Because the river valleys which are flooded tend to be fertile, these people are almost always agriculturally successful (even if monetarily poor),[8] and they are often tribal minorities with cultures and traditions irreplaceably tied to their land. The electric power that the dams produce almost never benefits the local people but is transported to the industrial centers, where the national government resides, primarily for the benefit of the state industries or multinational corporations that are situated there.

The misery these projects produce for the local population is justified by their presumed benefit to the greater economy; they are seen as economic imperatives in much the same way the slave trade a century or more ago was deemed necessary for the economic progress of Western nations.

This latter-day moral equivalent of the slave trade stops short of selling the men, women, and children it has claimed mastery over; today's slave traders are not rogues in sailing garb but often well meaning politicians and bureaucrats in pinstriped suits. Nevertheless, the effect of this human trade — the forcible removal of peoples from their homeland to satisfy commercial interests elsewhere — is in many ways the same. As explained by the Anti-Slavery Society, a London-based organization which dates back to the emancipation movement of British slaves in the 1800s and today still works to fight abuses outlawed by the United Nations as "practices similar to slavery",

> Threats commonly faced by indigenous peoples throughout the world include dispossession of

> land, flooding of land through hydroelectric schemes, deforestation and the consequent damage to traditional agriculture, armed forces carrying out the policies of distant central governments, desecration of places of worship and ethnocide, the destruction of a culture. The enemies, wittingly or not, of indigenous peoples are multinational companies, international funding agencies and governments bent on 'development' at all costs.[9]

The West was able to finance its slave trade itself, but most Third World governments have no such means. As a result, they have turned to the West's international financiers to see their projects through: foreign aid agencies like the World Bank, the United States Agency for International Development, and the Canadian International Development Agency; national commercial banks like Chase Manhattan and the Canadian Imperial Bank of Commerce; export promotion bodies like the Export-Import Bank in the U.S. and the Export Development Corporation in Canada.[10] In effect, these international bodies are financing national governments against local populations.

THERE IS A SCHOOL of thought that people in the Third World cannot handle democracy, and that there is no alternative to relieving their poverty other than for the West to provide whatever help it can to the Third World governments, in the hope that some of it will reach the masses of people. This approach has few adherents among the populations of the Third World, who consider themselves able to look after their own affairs.

Westerners think "democracy is too good for us," said Mario Vargas Llosa, the noted Peruvian novelist.[11] Westerners "cultivate a good conscience for themselves," they never notice "the millions of men and women who are able and yearning to live in a democracy....what I want for my country and Latin America is the kind of civilization and well-being that brought liberty to the West."

Llosa complains that the West's "stereotypes [which] show only generals who are rich or revolutionaries who are angelic" rule out democratic government by a politically empowered population, and he is joined by other critics around the world who want political power to be shared. Chadli Klibi, the Tunisian head of the Arab League, believes that Arabs must learn that development can't be bought, that it won't work without political progress.[12] Luis Burstin, a former Costa Rican Secretary of Information, blames foreign aid for helping to foster revolution. It isn't poverty and social injustice that provoke Latin revolutions, he says, but the freezing of political power which blocks access to emerging groups. Without political reform, no amount of foreign aid can break the vicious circle: "None of the countries of the region have the means to distribute this money....as a result, most of our wealth is left in the hands of a very small part of the population."[13] For this reason, the Kissinger Commission's plan to give $8.4 billion in economic aid to Central America over the next five years is doomed to fail, he says, pointing to the previous three years, during which almost twice that amount was funneled out of Central America to buy foreign real estate or to be deposited in foreign banks.

El Salvador's Planning Minister, Manuel Antonio Robles, acknowledges that the foreign aid dollars go to a few wealthy people, as did El Salvador's former Economy Minister, who admitted that aid has obviously had "very little effect on poverty."[14] The recent history of foreign aid to this mostly undemocratic corner of the world has been a sorry one, with aid, especially from the U.S., increasing rapidly while the economies of these countries has been deteriorating.

Where the population is left to its own devices, either because the central government is more democratic or because it does not have the means to control the outlying areas, the economy seems to fare better. Undemocratic Tanzania, which receives the most foreign aid of any African country — an amount greater than its tax revenues and one-and-a-half times its export earnings — has had well meaning but highly centralized policies that have devastated production, helped to spread famine, and forcibly uprooted millions. More democratic India, which receives aid equal to 16.8 percent of tax revenues and 31.2 percent of export earnings, has a far more vibrant economy.[15]

Democracy, which means no more than citizens having a meaningful say in the affairs of their society, need not be equated with Western systems of democracy: societies around the world, including tribal societies governed by chiefs or village elders, have historically shared power to a great extent, with decisions being made in public meetings, and with local leaders granted their authority by the people they governed. The creation of artificial national borders by the Third World's colonial rulers produced supra-governments that often resulted in less democratic societies ruled by more distant and aloof leaders. But these recent disruptions are no indication that people in the Third World don't desire a say in the affairs of their society, or that democracy is not embedded in them as a deeply held value.

Delivering democracy in a CARE package may not be possible, but neither should it be possible for the Western governments and their agencies, in the name of progress, to so routinely and so counter-productively deliver foreign aid that makes the destruction of democratic processes possible.

# PART I

# Dispossessing the Disenfranchised: The Foreign Aid Myths

# 1

## *Foreign aid is humanitarian and does not violate human rights*

"There is a greater good to be derived from the setting up of the dam .... and each group has to be willing to make some sacrifice for the benefit of the entire society."
— Dr. Placido Mapa, Philippine Minister of National Planning and Development, in a film interview, 1982.

"The government says dams are for development. Development for what? To us development is for people. But in constructing the dams, development is going to be achieved at our expense."
— A Kalinga spokesman, quoted in *Invasions: Tribal Peoples and the Struggle for Their Land,* 1984.

WHILE FOREIGN AID may be provided for humanitarian reasons, it often has an effect that we least expect and that we least intend. Major development projects, and in this energy projects are among the worst offenders, almost invariably involve the forced relocation of communities, relocations that literally deprive people of their physical and social environment and, in all too many cases, of their human rights as enshrined in the International Bill of Human Rights. Although not as popularly known as the human right to be free from arbitrary arrest, torture, and execution, which Amnesty International and others have championed so well, the rights of ethnic minorities to their own culture and religion and the rights of all peoples to their own means of subsistence and to their natural wealth and resources are equally protected in the International Bill of Human Rights.[1]

> *Article 1*
>
> All peoples may, for their own ends, freely dispose of their natural wealth and resources without prejudice to any obligations arising out of international economic cooperation, based upon the principle of mutual benefit, and international law. In no case may a people be deprived of its own means of subsistence.[2]
>
> *Article 25*
>
> Nothing in the present Covenant shall be interpreted as impairing the inherent right of all peoples to enjoy and utilize fully and freely their natural wealth and resources.[3]
>
> *Article 27*
>
> In those States in which ethnic, religious or linguis-

> tic minorities exist, persons belonging to such minorities shall not be denied the right, in community with other members of their group, to enjoy their own culture, to profess and practise their own religion, or to use their own language.[4]

Despite this protection, thousands of development projects have arbitrarily deprived millions of people in the Third World of their right to the physical and social environment on which they have depended for their subsistence, causing great suffering and even death.

The most clear-cut examples of such human rights violations involve tribal societies whose particular economic, social, political, and religious systems have evolved to suit their specific habitats. Transferring these systems intact to another piece of land is, in practice, impossible.

Agricultural techniques that have been adapted over generations for one region may wreak environmental havoc when applied to another region. Social relationships tied to a particular region are more likely to be dissolved than transferred when relocation takes place. Religious rights are similarly non-transferable: flooding the ancestral lands of indigenous peoples in the name of development is as unthinkable to them as flooding Salt Lake City would be to Mormons, flooding the Vatican would be to Catholics, flooding Mecca would be to Moslems, and flooding Jerusalem would be to Christians, Moslems or Jews.

Unthinkable or not, human rights violations such as these are often unavoidable byproducts of the grandiose energy development schemes of Third World governments, many of which are backed by financing from the Western foreign aid agencies.[5] The Ten-Year Energy Program of the Philippine Government, under which 31 hydroelectric dams are scheduled to be built in lands presently occupied by tribal minorities, provides a disturbing example of the extent to which foreign aid projects can be disruptive, and the extraordinary measures that can be required to complete them.

Major foreign aid donors participating in this program include the United States Agency for International Development, the World Bank, and the Asian Development Bank although, according to the Anti-Slavery Society, this program "threatens the mountain homes of many minorities and a total of one-and-a-half to two million people."[6]

To carry out the program, the Philippine government felt it necessary to enact legislation giving what amounts to police powers to the country's electric utility: it has been granted the authority to restrict or prohibit farming within the watershed of a proposed dam and the authority to relocate residents to areas outside the watershed.

One part of the electrification megaproject, the Chico River Basin Development Project in the northern province of Luzon, fomented a long and destructive struggle between the Philippine government and the 85,000 members of the Kalinga and Bontoc tribes, and became the *cause célèbre* of a worldwide movement to defend indigenous rights. Originally financed by loans from the World Bank and West Germany, the government utility began surveying four proposed dam sites on the Chico River in 1974. When the numerous appeals of the Bontoc and Kalingas to stop the flooding of their 7,000 acres were dismissed by the Philippine government, these tribal people resorted to attacks on the survey crews and to dismantling their campsites and equipment. The survey work eventually had to be completed from the air.

As the resistance to these projects escalated so too did the government's military activity: early on, check points were established along access roads and by 1981 full-scale military operations were launched with troops backed by air support. Since 1981, a 700-man battalion has been stationed in the area to reinforce a 150-man provincial force.

Ambushes by the local people and retaliation by the government troops, which has escalated to bombing, have become common. Deaths have been rising on both sides and innocent villagers have been terrorized by military atrocities. Violence aside, the villagers have suffered from restrictions on their farming activities: they are allowed to tend their fields for only six hours a day and only if they secure permits. The livelihood of these once-prosperous people has been so seriously disrupted that they face severe food shortages. This war of attrition being waged for the sake of these dams is calculated to break these "people of the mountains," according to Charles Drucker, an American anthropologist who lived in the Chico River Valley.[7]

For generations the Bontocs and Kalingas have successfully maintained their distinctive communities because they had retained control over their lands. Gone with their right to their land will be their model form of agriculture which, despite centuries of highly intensive farming in terraces carved into mountains, shows no signs of exhausting the soil. "For generation after generation of highland farmers, they have produced consistently abundant harvests without chemical fertilizers, herbicides, insecticides, or elaborate farm machinery," said Drucker. "Impeccable maintenance and the complex ecology of the pondfield combined to make the Bontoc and Kalinga subsistence system stable, self-perpetuating, inherently conservative, and nearly indestructible."[8]

The government insists that the Kalingas and Bontocs rebuild their terraces in relocation sites further up the mountains, but these plans hold no hope of success for these tribal peoples. As explained by one Bontoc:

> if we thought those sites were all right, we would have started colonies there ourselves a long time ago. Some of us did try, actually, but with no success. Building rice terraces is not simply a matter of putting up stone walls. The paddies have to be watered, nursed along, coaxed into bloom, but this takes years, generations even, before they start producing well.[9]

Equally important to the physical well-being and the social order of these people has been the spiritual role of the land:

> Now we are asked to allow our dead to be covered over by the waters of Chico. This is an impossible request. Separated from our dead, we will die. We may as well remain here and drown in the same waters that will wipe them out forever. The government assures us it will spare no effort nor expense to disinter the dead, to remove their remains to new and better sites. It does not understand. The very soil we tread on — this is the dust of our fathers.[10]

Even if the physical and spiritual value of the land were negotiable, any faith the people might have in the government's promise to relocate them has been poisoned by previous dislocations of other Filipino peoples by other hydro dams.

Two hundred Ibaloi families who were displaced by the

nearby Ambuklao dam in the 1950s were promised $100 per acre for their flooded lands. Few received it. Relocation sites proposed by the government turned out to be occupied, or on the ancestral lands of other tribes, or on a remote, malaria-infested island at the other end of the Philippine archipelago. Twenty years later, the Ibaloi were still to be relocated.[11]

Nine thousand Ilongot people displaced in the early 1970s by the Pantabangan dam, which was jointly financed by the Philippine government, the U.S. Agency for International Development, and the World Bank, were moved from a highly productive lowland area to an ecologically degraded upland region. To make matters worse, these people have no title to their new land, only "squatting permits" issued by the government on an annual basis. With no incentive to make permanent improvements to their surroundings, the resettled villagers are producing less than one third their previous yields of rice. Those who could not feed their families were forced to seek employment either as farm laborers or by collecting and selling firewood.[12]

Such treatment did not escape the Kalingas and Bontocs who "have of our own accord quietly gone to check on the government's performance at Pantabangan, Binga, and Ambuklao regarding the promises made to the former inhabitants of those places. At Pantabangan, we saw a people without a will to live. They were still crying over the loss of their land. At Ambuklao we spoke with the householders who, up till now, are still waiting for promised compensation for destroyed property. How can we deal with a government that promises everything but whose word cannot be trusted?"[13]

The effects of mass relocation are rarely documented in a systematic way by official sources — usually the only records available are the anecdotal ones of the Bontocs and Kalingas and other affected peoples.

But in the case of the Kariba Dam in Zimbabwe (then Southern Rhodesia), which was funded by the World Bank in 1956, two independent researchers, Elizabeth Colson and Thayer Scudder, monitored the effects of mass relocation over a 17-year period. Their study, probably the most extensive one of its kind ever undertaken, concluded that "for the large majority of any population, compulsory relocation is a traumatic experience which causes multi-dimensional stress .... it is hard to imagine a more dramatic way to illustrate impotence than to forcibly eject people from a preferred habitat against their will."[14]

At first, the researchers discovered, the Tonga and Batonka tribes who lived on both sides of the Zambezi River tried to resist the relocation. After people were killed by the resettlement authorities the resistance abated, and the relocation began. But to the surprise of the officials in charge of the resettlement, when the time came to fill the reservoir that would form Lake Kariba they realized that they had not set aside enough land to relocate the 56,000 people who were being displaced. What ensued, according to Scudder, was "a crash and tension-ridden program to move the people before inundation."[15]

When the move appeared imminent, the resettlement authorities told the Tonga and Batonka not to plant crops that could not be harvested before the move. But the authorities were unable to meet their deadlines, and the move had to be postponed several times, leaving the population without its crops, underfed, and dependent on food relief.

When the Tonga and Batonka, who had once taken the water they needed freely from the river, arrived at their resettlement site they found that they had been given land short on water, especially clean drinking water. The result was numerous deaths from dysentery and other diseases spread by contaminated water that particularly strike populations suffering from protein deficiencies. A decade later, the diseases were still rampant[16] and two decades later the Tonga were still dependent on outside sources for food.[17]

The human rights abuses that occurred in the name of foreign aid to the 56,000 Tonga and Batonka at the Kariba Dam and to the 85,000 Bontocs and Kalingas in the Philippines are not isolated incidents — they occur over and over again in many parts of the world, with only the names and numbers changing.[18] Neither are they unique to countries with poor human rights records — they have occurred on a comparable scale in Third World countries like Ghana and Sri Lanka, which have had relatively good human rights records, and on a smaller scale in Western countries like Canada and the U.S., which are among the most democratic of countries.[19]

In most cases, the affected populations have endured hardships far beyond what their national governments imagined because the resettlement plans did not proceed according to schedule; yet the sheer enormity of the projects and the speed with which they were implemented guaranteed that the schedules would not be met. In most cases, because a shroud of secrecy hangs over these projects, the affected populations have been denied the right to public hearings that would question so much as how they would be moved, or how much compensation they were entitled to, let alone the rationale justifying these human rights abuses.

But in all cases, the human rights abuses occurred because of the predominant view that it is acceptable for a few to suffer for the sake of national economic development.

Because Third World governments, and their Western

financiers, do not recognize the rights of peoples to their means of subsistence, to their natural wealth, and to their culture, they will continue to be besieged with pleas like those of the T'Boli people of the Philippines to the Asian Development Bank:

> The proposed dam will flood our most precious land and destroy our food and source of livelihood .... In all this, we have never been directly approached, advised or informed regarding the planning of the dam. Do we not have rights? Are we not also Filipino citizens capable of planning for our future? .... We do think that real development has to be realized with the free participation of the common people no matter how poor they are.[20]

In the name of progress, the human rights of people around the world are violated. Some say there is no choice — that some people must inevitably be sacrificed so that development projects which will better the lot of the majority of the poor may proceed. In the long run, they claim, it will all be for the good.

# 2

## *Eventually, the billions we're spending on our energy aid will pay off for the Third World's poor*

"Indians of our Country, beneath your bare feet Panamanian copper is waiting to be converted into thousands of millions of dollars for the country, its children, for you and yours."
— From a 1979 series of government ads published in Panama's national press, exhorting Indians to give up their opposition to the hydro dam and roads required to develop the country's copper mines.

"The consequences .... have been that there is more electricity for the industries of the country, but for the Kunas and the Chocoes there is less land, less agricultural produce, lower income, and further marginalization."
— The Guaymi Indians of Panama are skeptical that their lot will be any better. From the Guaymi Presiding Committee, Panama, 1980.

THAT FOREIGN AID can bring hardship to the Third World's poor becomes explicable when its function is understood: foreign aid is not necessarily designed to reach the Third World's poor directly — it is not considered an end in itself but merely a means to an end. And whether the means justify the ends is a matter that has always been in dispute.

In the energy area, almost all foreign aid is used to fund business ventures for governments, not products for people. Unlike the television portrayal of foreign aid, in which a Third World family might receive temporary help in the form of powdered milk or wheat, energy aid is not designed to provide a family with comparable commodities like firewood or oil. Instead, most energy aid is intended to provide lasting benefits by helping Third World governments explore for oil or, more often, build electrical facilities. The oil that the government finds or the electricity that it produces is then used to further whatever ends the government has planned. In the worst of cases, the ends are ridden with corruption and very few benefit. In the best of cases, the ends are noble — spurring industries and providing jobs — and more may benefit.

International aid agencies usually fund these energy projects not through outright grant but by low-interest loans. For the multilateral aid agencies like the World Bank, these loans are taken very seriously, because they need to be repaid for the agencies to remain in business. They generally are repaid.[1] For example, the World Bank, which lends more money than any other aid agency, has made loans totalling over $100 billion without any defaults.[2]

This impressive record has not come about by accident. Like any commercial bank, the World Bank wants to be sure that its debtors (those who receive its aid loans) have the means to repay the loans before they are extended for any business venture. By definition, this excludes loans to the poor. This also tends to exclude loans for risky business ventures such as those that would provide products of use to the poor, because in the absence of a market with purchasing power the venture could collapse, leaving the loan unpaid. But business ventures that have a guaranteed source of revenue, such as electrical stations that will supply mining or manufacturing operations, are good credit risks and therefore good candidates to receive foreign aid. As a result, energy aid funds are generally used to satisfy commercial interests which in turn receive an almost assured profit through the favorable terms they are able to negotiate. Companies such as Kaiser and Reynolds in Ghana, Amax in Zimbabwe, and Alcan in Guinea have obtained contracts for electricity at rates as low as one-tenth world rates.[3] They have structured their deals to insure a rate of return satisfactory to their shareholders, and they have had the comfort of knowing the contracts will be enforced by the foreign aid agencies, which are themselves determined to have their loans repaid.

Sometimes, rates charged for electricity can be renegotiated only with the agreement of the aid agency that finances the electricity project. Under the terms of the World Bank's agreement with Ghana, the bank, which is a major financier, is entitled to demand immediate repayment of loans if Ghana unilaterally changes the terms of its contract with Kaiser and Reynolds[4] — a power that insures the stability they need.

The poor have no such insurance policy from foreign aid agencies, nor any prospects that the foreign aid project will pay off for them. They do not share in the cheap electricity being made available to attract industry, only in the hardship that is its byproduct. As put by Philippine President Marcos in a candid *Fortune* magazine advertisement designed to attract foreign investment, "to attract companies .... like yours .... we have felled mountains, razed jungles, filled swamps, moved rivers, relocated towns, and in their place built power plants, dams, roads .... All to make it easier for you and your business to do business here."[5]

Marcos's attempt to rapidly industrialize his country through major energy development projects failed to benefit the poor, as did other attempts in other parts of the world.

Jane Jacobs, in her landmark book, *Cities and the Wealth of Nations*, describes unsuccessful attempts to stimulate development in poor or stagnant regions, such as the Tennessee River Valley in the United States, Southern Italy, and Ghana's Volta River Valley.[6] Each region, aided by either national or international subsidies, built major facilities to lure distant industries. For the Tennessee and Volta River valleys, cheap electricity was their greatest asset, but although the cheap electricity benefitted the transplanted industries, the regions themselves did not prosper but remained stagnant. Jacobs, and numerous others, conclude that the poor are not ultimately served by these foreign aid gifts.

The futility of expecting progress to flow from these energy projects is verified by one of the few detailed, after-the-fact evaluations ever conducted of one of these forced industrialization projects — David Hart's renowned study of the same Volta River Project that Jacobs had examined.[7] The hopes of the Ghanaian government in the 1950s were high: "With this hydroelectric power in our country," they exulted, "many factories will be established and we shall be in a position to manufacture most of our commodities. The project will help to solve so many problems, such as unemployment, for men and women will get enough work to do."[8] But Hart's assessment 20 years later shows "a zero or negligible influence from the Volta River Project on Ghana's industrialization."

"Undoubtedly," Hart says, "the production and distribution of electricity is efficiently carried out," in particular, to Kaiser Aluminum and Reynolds Metals. "But to look beyond the provision of electricity: the government's aim in setting up the project was to achieve a significant measure of industrialization. This does not seem to have occurred."

Promises by Third World governments, or by Western aid agencies, that major energy aid projects will spur a thriving industrial economy whose benefits will trickle down to the poor are hollow. Yet the myth that these projects contribute to the general welfare continues to be asserted in the First World as confidently as in the Third.

In an unqualified defense of hydroelectric dams in 1984, Allan MacEachen, as Canadian Secretary of State for External Affairs, unequivocally claimed that hydro dams relieve unemployment:

> Industries in the Third World are major employers just as they are elsewhere. The Third World has problems of unemployment often exacerbated by severe underemployment. The situation is often chronic in the cities and, without the energy provided to support industries, it would be considerably worse.[9]

He then proceeded to further claim that hydro dams provide numerous other side benefits "on a huge scale: river navigation; fishing industries; flood control; opportunities for a tourism industry; a transport link across the dam; water regulation for irrigation; agriculture on the newly stabilized riverbanks; reduction of crippling oil import bills; and so on." This catalog of riches more resembles the fantasies of the Minister than the history of these projects, because evaluations of how they have worked out five or ten years after their completion are rarely undertaken by either Third World governments or foreign aid agencies: all that these official bodies do is prepare reports listing the intended benefits of the dams, and it is these intended benefits that MacEachen was reciting.

When independently scrutinized, with frightening regularity the expected benefits of these giant hydro schemes turn out to have been greatly exaggerated, and their costs — most often their social and environmental costs — turn out to have been either underestimated or ignored altogether. Drawbacks, such as the number of livelihoods lost because of a project, are not weighed against the number of jobs which are expected to be created.[10]

In Ghana, no one knows what happened to most of the 80,000 people who lost their livelihood when they were thrown off their land to make way for the hydro dam. Some of them, and some in other parts of the country, obtained jobs they would otherwise not have had: 2,000 people were employed at the Kaiser and Reynolds aluminum smelter and 10,000 additional people were able to fish for their livelihoods in Lake Volta, which the dam created.

The fishing industry was an unexpected success; the side benefits expected in agriculture, navigation, transportation, and elsewhere, according to Hart, were unexpected disasters.

The Volta River Project's main purpose — to produce electricity for profit — also must be termed a disaster.[11] Even in good years, when water levels in Lake Volta were high, revenue from the dam barely covered its carrying charges; and during bad years, when drought reduced the amount of water power available for sale, the dam became a major foreign exchange drain.[12]

One casualty of this revenue shortfall was irrigation for agricultural lands, which was intended to improve the lot of farmers in Ghana.[13] But ironically, experience in other countries shows that the farmers may have been fortunate, because irrigation schemes are as likely as not to be failures.

The Indian Planning Commission has discovered that India's huge investments in irrigation have produced disappointingly low returns for the farmer: only one third the expected grain yield.[14] More threateningly, because the irrigation canals drain poorly, water tables have risen in some areas by as much as 25 feet within ten years, boosting the salinity and alkalinity of soils and jeopardizing at least one quarter of India's 100 million acres of irrigated land.[15] Throughout the world's arid zones, improperly designed and managed irrigation systems are turning one-and-a-quarter million acres of irrigated land into desert every year — roughly the same area that is newly irrigated each year.[16]

This is not the only example of how the pace of development can accelerate while progress itself stays at a standstill, or even slides backward: hydro dams, because they force the poor to search for alternatives to their agriculturally rich valleys and plains where none exist, often have the same effect.

Evicted from their valleys, the poor move either into nearby forests, which they clear to farm, or onto smaller or less fertile plots in more marginal areas. In these new lands, which they usually farm under crowded conditions and where they are always fearful of being uprooted again, their traditional care in husbanding the soil often falls by the wayside. When this occurs, the soil soon becomes farmed to exhaustion, and the poor must then cut down more forests for more land to farm.[17]

This cutting of trees is a major cause of deforestation, and with deforestation comes the loss of topsoil and the spreading of more deserts. That means less food, less fuel, and the continuation of a downward spiral that causes the destruction of the local environment upon which the poor, and their descendants, depend.

As a final irony, the topsoil lost from the land goes into the river basins and ends up filling the dam reservoirs, cutting the useful life of the dams by up to one half. Then, whatever industrial development depends on power from these dams will have to either stop or find some new source of power. These dams, which are considered but a means to an end, will no longer be a means, and neither will the ends be secured. But the river valleys on which thousands had depended for their livelihoods will have been destroyed, yielding no more harvests and providing no more power.

# 3

## *Whatever else happens, developing renewable resources, such as hydroelectricity, means that our gift will last forever*

"In a world suffering from inflation and fossil-fuel depletion, hydropower offers stable prices and permanence .... The fact that water resources exist in abundance in many of the world's poorest regions and nations places hydropower high on the global development agenda."
— *Rivers of Energy*, Worldwatch Institute, June 1981.

"Big dam schemes do seem to contain within them seeds which lead to their own long-term demise."
— John Madeley in "Dams with faint praise," in *Development Forum*, April 1984.

THE PELIGRE HYDROELECTRIC dam in Haiti was hailed just one generation ago as a great boon to the Haitian economy. Thanks to this inexhaustible source of power, which would fuel industries in and around the capital city of Port-au-Prince, prosperity was just around the corner.

What opposition this dam might have aroused among those whose valley was flooded would not have been taken seriously by the majority of the population. Here was a chance for Haiti to have lasting benefits: those who would put their own selfish interests ahead of the national interests must surely have been quickly dismissed.

Today, because it is filling up with silt, the Peligre dam is so incapacitated that cities are blacked out for as much as twelve hours daily. The government has been looking for a way of replacing the power lost at Peligre, and it thinks it has found it in flooding two sections of the Artibonite River Valley, which is dubbed the "breadbasket of Haiti."[1] A generation from now, after this prime agricultural land has been retired, the government may look for more valleys to flood.

The myth that hydro dams, like diamonds, are forever has led the world's foreign aid agencies to promote dam construction above all other energy projects.[2] The enormity of this mistake is only now beginning to sink in.

The Ambuklao Dam in the Philippines has silted up so fast that its lifespan has been reduced to 32 years from the 60 originally predicted.[3] Kenya's largest hydroelectric complex, Kamburu, is receiving almost six million tons of soil a year, which has reduced its useful lifespan to under 30 years.[4] Numerous other reservoirs in Kenya have filled with sediment in 15 or 20 years, severely reducing their ability to support electricity generation, provide water for irrigation, or control floods.[5]

Studies of 17 major reservoirs in India show them to be silting up at three times the expected rate. The giant Tehri Dam, now under construction on the Bhagirathi River, is expected to last only 30 to 40 years instead of the 100-year minimum initially planned.[6]

Short-lived projects like these are the norm but by no means the worst. In Colombia the Anchicaya Dam, completed in 1955, lost one quarter of its storage capacity in its first 21 months of operation and 20 years later had lost 80 percent of its seven million cubic yard capacity to siltation.[7] The Sanmenxia Dam in the Yellow River Basin of China was completed in 1960, but had to be decommissioned in 1964 because so much sediment accumulated in its reservoir that the riverbank eroded and threatened to flood the City of Xian. The Laoying Reservoir, also in China, filled with sediment before the dam was completed.[8]

This extraordinarily rapid accumulation of silt behind the reservoirs should not have taken the hydro engineers by surprise. But it did because most of the hydro dams built in the Third World in the last 30 years were built with Western money by Western-trained engineers whose experience and knowledge ill-prepared them for building hydro dams in the Third World. Due to natural factors, such as climate, relief, geology, and vegetation; and to man-made factors such as cattle ranching, agriculture, and logging, the runoff of soil into the river systems of most of the Third World[9] is generally much higher than the runoff into the river systems of the industrialized world. The rivers of Asia which flow to the sea between Korea and Pakistan alone contribute nearly 50 percent of the total sediment transported to the world's oceans. Ranking first, second, and third in terms of sediment loads is the Ganges/Brahmaputra River System in the Indian subcontinent, the Yellow River in China, and the Amazon in South America.[10] Siltation, which in the West usually occurs at too low a rate to be a factor to the dam builders, becomes the overriding factor in many other parts of the world.

Not only are these large hydro dams non-renewable themselves, but they also reduce the renewability of their river valleys, and thereby the self-sufficiency of the entire region.

By interfering with the natural flow of the river and trapping the nutrient-rich silt in the reservoirs instead of letting it wash it over the river banks during the annual flooding, the dams deprive the flood plains of the nutrients needed to maintain their agricultural productivity. As a result, regions that now have reservoirs for hydroelectricity usually become dependent on petrochemical-based fertilizers to replenish their soil[11] and on man-made irrigation systems to replace the lost irrigation of the annual floods. Without the soil's natural replenishment, and with its more intensive use under modern agricultural systems, come a decrease in the area's ability to regulate itself naturally, and an increase in the amount of topsoil that silts up in the riverbed and eventually destroys the dam. In the end, the river provides neither hydroelectricity nor irrigation nor fertilization nor flood control for its river valley.

The intrusion of these dams into ecologically sensitive areas upsets the existing equilibrium to claim a human toll as well. According to Alan Meltzer, a tropical disease expert at the International Development Research Centre in Ottawa, the practice of building hydroelectric dams and irrigation projects in the Third World is the "way you create a malaria problem."[12] In addition to malaria, which today affects 800 million people and kills one million children younger than two years of age every year, bilharzia, a disease which thrives in the still waters of irrigation canals and dam reservoirs, debilitates some 200 million people.[13]

Despite the devastating consequences that so often accompany these dams, they are being built on an unprecedented scale. The World Bank estimates that $100 billion will be spent in the Third World on hydro projects over the next two decades, much of it to build dams so large that they are almost outside our experience. The Grand Coulee Dam on the Columbia River, for example, is 550 feet high. In the 1980s alone, 33 dams over 500 feet high are slated to be completed in the Third World; by the year 2000, if plans proceed as scheduled, virtually all of the world's major river valleys will have been irrevocably altered by dams.[14]

Some foreign aid agencies, particularly AID in the U.S., have abandoned large hydro dams because of their failure to promote development. But others, Canada's International Development Agency and Britain's Overseas Development Administration among them, continue to push hydroelectric development as a gift that keeps on giving.[15]

The reason for this preference cannot be explained entirely by ignorance of the terminal nature of these gifts. Unenlightened self-interest on the part of the governments that provide aid and the corporations that deliver it also plays a role.

# 4

## *We can kill two birds with one stone by giving the Third World our products, boosting our own economy and helping the needy abroad*

"For our own benefit as well as [the Third World's, we will] help Canadian firms to provide additional goods and services in support of Third World development."
— Marc Lalonde, Canada's Finance Minister, in the Budget Speech, Feb. 15, 1984.

"The people of Sri Lanka today could build this project faster than is being done now. There are too many foreign contracts. The people have not made it their own."
— D. N. Fernando, official with the Mahaweli Authority, quoted in "Harnessing Sri Lanka's Nile," *Christian Science Monitor*.

CANADA, WHICH IS GENERALLY numbered among the countries considered to have a good foreign aid record, is one of the world's chief proponents of large hydro dams for the Third World: over half of Canada's energy aid dollars has been dedicated to hydroelectric systems, and with the exception of the few Canadians who are aware of the problems that can be associated with these dams, most would endorse this type of foreign aid.

Most would also endorse their government's requirement that Canadian engineers and Canadian contractors design and build the dams. They would see little sense in allowing American or West German dam builders to get the business when Canadians could do the job just as well. This is how foreign aid is promoted in Canada — as something which is good for the Third World and good for Canada because the aid is tied to Canadian goods and services.

On the surface, the logic seems unassailable; scratch the surface and tied aid loses its luster. Compared to aid with no strings attached (which itself has a disappointing record), tied aid can be justified neither as a boon to a receiving country nor as a boon to a donor country like Canada.

From the Third World country's point of view, it can never be better off receiving a gift of Canadian products instead of the cash required to buy them. With cash it can shop anywhere in the world for the goods and services that most closely meet its own needs at the best available price. When Canadian goods are too expensive, the Third World country would be able to purchase the goods elsewhere, and save the balance of its cash for another need. When Canadians don't produce a particular product, the Third World country would not be forced to settle for something that almost does the job.

But Canada won't give foreign aid to countries in the form of cash; Canada wants to make sure the Third World buys Canadian.

The cost to the Third World of this conditional generosity varies in estimate. According to a study by the Canadian

Treasury Board,[1] Third World aid recipients pay 15 percent to 20 percent more than necessary for a development project financed with tied Canadian aid. According to the World Bank-sponsored Commission on International Development, the cost is over 20 percent,[2] and according to Maurice Strong, the first president of the Canadian International Development Agency, the federal government's foreign aid arm, the cost is closer to 25 percent.[3]

The cost in terms of dollars, though considerable to impoverished countries, may be dwarfed by the cost of being forced to choose a technology that would otherwise not be chosen. Canada, matched only by the U.S., has the world's worst record in using energy efficiently for almost any given task.[4]

Canadian tractors given to a Third World country, as a result, tend to increase that country's long-term dependence on imported petroleum fuels. So do Canadian transportation systems, food production systems, and numerous other foreign aid projects Canada offers.[5] Canadian advice tends to be debilitating as well. When Canada sends consultants to the Third World their recommendations mirror their training and experience in Canada, whose industrial economy grew up on cheap energy, and whose energy systems are the product of a myriad of uniquely Canadian political decisions.

Among Canada's many foreign aid consultants are Hydro-Québec and Ontario Hydro, provincially owned electrical utilities that have received contracts worth millions of dollars over the years from the federal government to advise Third World governments on how to set up their own electrical systems.[6] These utilities are abnormally large, they exercise monopolies over larger territories than any other utility in the non-Communist world, and they have acquired these gigantic proportions by forcing competing producers of power out of business and replacing their small-scale facilities with large-scale systems. When Hydro-Québec or Ontario Hydro offers advice, it does not emphasize the benefits of having a small or decentralized electricity system.

Neither does the advice of other Canadian engineers, who have earned their living in large part by servicing the needs of Canada's giant utilities. It has been two generations since Canada's engineers have had to understand the workings of small utility systems.[7]

Canadian engineers understandably have a tendency to think big, and as a result Third World governments receiving their advice tend to adopt big systems, such as big hydroelectric dams, whether bigness is required or not. In this way, huge and wholly inappropriate systems have been adopted in the Third World at Canada's behest. Some of these systems might have been adopted had Canada's aid not been tied — there are many reasons for Third World leaders to want centralized systems and grandiose projects — but tying aid virtually guarantees that what is offered gets accepted, because the alternative for the Third World government would be no system at all. Tied aid, from the Third World government's perspective, amounts to "take it or leave it."

But from the perspective of the giving country, tied aid also has severe shortcomings because it inflates the cost of delivering foreign aid. In Canada's case, where the cost is inflated by 15 percent to 25 percent, the one billion-odd dollars that were tied in 1983 were diminished in value by between $150 million and $250 million. Canadian taxpayers thus became losers as well: they could have provided the Third World with gifts of equal worth at a tax saving of a quarter of a billion dollars.

This substantial loss to Canadian taxpayers is not balanced by comparable gains elsewhere.

Based on the Treasury Board figures, tying foreign aid to Canadian products seriously undermines Canada's aid effort for only minimal benefit to the Canadian economy as a whole: only about $10 million in profit at home would have been lost with the untying of Canadian aid for the 1974 fiscal year, the period it studied.[8]

As for the more technical concerns of economists, such as the balance of payments situation, untying aid would have worsened it but too little to "have any significant effect on the exchange rate."[9] The "often-quoted argument in favor of tied aid" — that it helps Canadian industry penetrate foreign markets by being a loss leader — had no merit at all to the Treasury Board report, which bluntly said that "this argument has been dismissed." The report found that "there is no commercial or technological link" between the products Canada gives to the Third World and the products they later buy.[10] Even the service sector, primarily consulting engineers, does not provide an entry for future profits because Third World countries simply cannot afford to buy Canadian services at market rates. "Accordingly, services .... can only occasionally be exported without public or international financing."

These striking findings nevertheless understate the total cost of our self-interest. As the Treasury Board report stressed, "the cost that we have calculated minimizes the total cost of tied aid for the recipient countries, since it does not take into account the indirect costs incurred because these countries do not necessarily receive the kinds of goods and services that they need most urgently." A Third World country, in other words, may not need any of the energy systems available in Canada. Instead of limiting its choice to several undesirables, Canada could be giving Third World countries additional options by untying its aid and providing cash. Kenya, for example, might use the cash to relieve the energy crisis in its rural areas by purchasing biogas digesters from China instead of taking another hydroelectric facility from Canada to serve its urban industries.

Although Canada's electrical industry would be deprived of some aid business, the effect of this "lost sale" to Canada is not as bad as it seems. Canadian dollars would have gone to China instead of back to Canada, and the Chinese, who would now have them, might choose to spend them in Canada on another commodity, say communications equipment. Or the Chinese might choose to spend them in another country. (Canada's dollars would be worthless to the Chinese if their value were not claimed.)

Whether those dollars come back to Canada from China or from another country, sooner or later they will be used to claim goods from Canada, because Canada is the issuing country, and ultimately the only one responsible for exchanging its dollars for the goods and services they represent.[11]

In effect, what will have happened is this: instead of Canada's foreign aid dollars returning from Kenya to buy electrical products, they will be coming from China or any other country to buy communications equipment or any other Canadian product. The same number of Canadian dollars will have circulated, but the benefits will have been spread across Canada's economy, instead of having been limited to particular industries or to particular companies.

Those particular industries, the Treasury Board report tentatively concludes, are those industries which "profit from the monopolistic position in which tied aid has put them," and within these industries, a handful of companies appear to reap the lion's share of those monopoly benefits.

In the manufacturing sector, a mere 23 suppliers — primarily multinational corporations like General Electric,

Raytheon, and Westinghouse — accounted for 75 percent of the aid business. Tied aid here forced Third World countries to pay a penalty of at least 25 percent for the benefit of these corporations.

The engineering consulting industry also forced the Third World into paying a 25 percent surcharge. Half of the firms involved, according to the Treasury Board, were "characterized by a dependency on aid contracts and a lack of experience" in international markets. Sixteen consulting firms landed 56 percent of the $83.8 million spent by the Canadian International Development Agency for consulting services, while 21 consulting firms were found to be so uncompetitive that "if the contracts obtained through CIDA had been untied, these firms probably would not have received them, since they could not have successfully challenged their foreign competitors."

The Treasury Board's 1976 analysis has stood up well. In the following years, with the domestic market for large-scale industrial projects shrinking, these Canadian consulting firms have proved unable to penetrate international markets. Crippled by their inability to compete, they usually did not bother to even bid. In 1977, Canadian companies bid on only 2.3 percent of 7,200 tenders called by the World Bank. In 1978, the percentage of tenders for which bids were submitted dropped to 1.3 percent. Between 1973 and 1982, Canadian companies did not submit a single bid on more than 1,700 civil works contracts financed by the Asian Development Bank, with a total value of $1.4 billion.[12]

Tied aid is not good for a nation's overall welfare, but because this is generally not well recognized by the public most countries, to varying degrees, tie their aid. Among the industrialized countries of the Organization for Economic Cooperation and Development, Finland ties the least, only twelve percent of its foreign aid budget, and the United States ties relatively little, 32 percent. At the other end of the scale, Canada ties 65 percent of its foreign aid funds, twice as much as the U.S. and second only to Austria.[13]

This much corruption of the purpose of foreign aid is less attributable to the force of Canada's business lobby[14] than to the absence of an organized lobby that is able to present the case against tied aid to the Canadian public. Recognizing tied aid's failure, the federal government had pledged in 1975 to eliminate it, and a Parliamentary Task Force in 1980[15] wanted it reduced because "short-term commercial objectives should not be permitted to undermine the development purposes of the assistance program." In general terms, the public also agrees: according to a 1980 poll commissioned by CIDA,[16] over 90 percent of Canadians want their foreign aid to be given for humanitarian or moral reasons while only four percent thought it should be given in order to benefit Canadian business. But because the myth persists that tied aid can both be humanitarian and help business, the government found it expedient to ignore its pledge rather than risk the wrath of the business lobby when it stood to receive little credit from a disinterested public.

To the Third World country, the choice between tied aid and no aid is unenviable; to the Westerner, it does not seem so bad. Even second best products, to our way of thinking, must surely be better than anything they have. Besides, we reason, we have used our resources so well, acted so responsibly, while the Third World is the continuing author of its own failure.

# PART II

# The Dispossession Rationalized: Myths About Population and Resources

# 5

## *The Third World, with its billions of people, is straining the world's resources*

The global environment is threatened by "the impact poor people have on the earth's resources in their struggle to fulfil their most basic human needs. A hungry person couldn't care less about killing game in a protected area, fishing in an over-fished lake, cutting firewood on a steep slope ...."
— Dr. Russell Peterson, President of the National Audubon Society in the U.S., at a U.N. conference, June 15, 1982.

"I have never seen a case, and I challenge Dr. Peterson as a scientist to produce me one, where the poor have destroyed the environment. Those who consume less are dependent on the immediate environment, and they care for it."
— Anil Agarwal, Director of the Centre for Science and Environment in New Delhi, India, at the same conference.

IT IS THE WESTERN WORLD, with but a few hundred million people, which is straining the world's resources. Less than one fifth of the world's population — our fifth — consumes the lion's share of the world's oil, gas, coal, hydroelectricity, and other commercial fuels while the 70 percent of the world's population that lives in Third World countries uses only 13 percent.[1] The average North American consumes as much commercial energy as three Japanese, nine Mexicans, 16 Chinese, 53 Indians, 438 Malians, or 1,072 Nepalese. In fact, the energy used by the Third World for all purposes combined barely surpasses the amount of gasoline that the industrialized countries burn to move their automobiles.[2]

If everyone in the world consumed as much fuel as the average North American, the world would somehow need to find five times as much energy as it currently produces each year. Or, another way of looking at it, if everyone in the world used as much oil as the average North American, the world's remaining known reserves would last for only five years. Even if all the remaining ultimately recoverable oil reserves could be tapped, the world would only have enough for a further ten or eleven years.[3]

This lop-sided use of the world's energy resources is similar to the use of the world's other resources. According to United Nations data, the wealthiest ten percent in the world consume approximately 40 percent of the world's resources.[4] The figures are transposed for the poorest 40 percent of the world's population, who consume only ten percent of the world's resources. But even this meager share is in jeopardy as the search for resources by the world's richest people extends into the habitats of the poorest.

Nowhere is this phenomenon more dramatic than in the West's entry into the Third World's forests. As the West has been exhausting its own supplies of wood, and as standards to preserve its remaining forests have become more stringent, it has been turning increasingly to the Third World's forests to make up the shortfall.[5] The West has also been reaching

| Share of Consumption of World's Resources (%) | Wealth Level | Share of World's Population (%) |
|---|---|---|
| 40 | Very Rich | 10 |
| 30 | Rich | 20 |
| 20 | Poor | 30 |
| 10 | Very Poor | 40 |

into Third World forests — often at the invitation of Third World governments — for exotic species like mahogany and ebony, with the result that the carrying capacity of forests is being strained more and more. In 1950, the West imported only four million tons of tropical hardwood timber from the Third World. This figure soared to 50 million tons by 1980 and, according to World Bank projections, by the year 2000 the West could well be importing 100 million tons a year. In contrast to this 13-fold increase in the last 30 years, the use of tropical hardwood timber by the Third World itself barely doubled in the same period. Consumers in the industrialized countries now account for 60 percent of the total amount of timber cut down for commercial purposes in the Third World. This leaves a lot less for the Third World's population than in 1950, when only 20 percent of the cut was exported.[6]

In some countries the situation has reached crisis proportions. Unless present trends in the Philippines are reversed, the School of Forestry at the University of the Philippines predicts total denuding of the country's forests by the early 1990s. In the Ivory Coast, at the present rate of cutting — 2,000 square miles of tropical forest are logged each year while only twelve square miles are replanted — the nation's tropical forests will be eliminated this decade.[7]

Elsewhere, cash crop plantations or cattle-exporting ranches rival logging schemes as destroyers of forests.[8] In Central America, more than one quarter of all forests have been destroyed since 1960 to produce beef — 90 percent of which went to U.S. hamburger chains and pet food companies, which pay more than the Latin American peasant can afford. For this reason, despite the enormous increase in the amount of beef for export, less is affordable for the local people. In Guatemala, beef exports increased from zero to 15,000 tons per year in the last decade, but Guatemalans today eat 50 percent less beef.[9] Not only are the rainforests destroyed but food production suffers. In the pasturelands cleared from rainforest in the eastern Chiapas of Mexico, which has superior soil, the beef yield averages 54 pounds of meat per acre per year. In contrast, the traditional agricultural system of the area's indigenous inhabitants, the Lacandon Maya, produces up to 32,000 pounds of corn and 25,000 pounds of root and vegetable crops per acre per year in a sustainable cycle of five to seven consecutive years of planting followed by a fallow period of five to ten years. No such fallow period occurs in the case of cattle ranching, where the effect of overgrazing and torrential rains on the rainforest's soil soon turns pasture into eroded wastelands. Each head of cattle, which on newly cleared rainforest land requires two-and-a-half acres of land for grazing, needs an astonishing twelve to 17 acres within five to ten years. When this happens the rancher must find new tracts of cropland or rainforest to cut down for pasture. By most estimates, at least two thirds of Central America's arable land is now dedicated to cattle production and, without exception, these lands are less productive now than they were as forest lands cultivated by the rainforest Indians.[10]

This type of extraordinarily extensive use of the world's resources by the world's rich minority is a two-headed monster: it makes a disproportionately larger claim on the world's resources than its population would warrant and, at the same time, it forces the majority — the poor — to subsist on diminishing resources.

In most Third World countries, there are few unclaimed ecological niches that aren't vital to the sustenance of one community or another: forests provide families with their fuel, fodder, and food supplies; grasslands are essential to livestock-dependent nomadic peoples; and fish stocks are the main protein source for many communities throughout the Third World. When outside claims are made on these resources the communities that depend on them become dispossessed — they have no choice but either to move on, often to marginal lands, or to continue using what remains of their formerly sufficient resource. Either way they end up using what remains more intensively. This added pressure often tips the balance from a position of sustainable to unsustainable use, and renders sustainable systems unsustainable.

The traditional "slash-and-burn" method of clearing land for agriculture is often cited as a cause of Third World deforestation today, but it would not be harming the environment if the traditional extended fallow period — sometimes as long as 30 years — was allowed between times of cultivation. Instead farmers who find they have less and less land available to them are forced to shorten the fallow period and farm the land more frequently. According to the World Resources Institute, the farmer's quandary is all the more poignant because there is generally no feasible alternative to slash and burn in tropical rainforests which is ecologically sound. Attempts to replace it with modern methods of agriculture like annual cropping or crop rotations have been discouraging even when fertilizers, which are beyond the reach of most small farmers, are heavily used.[11]

The West's appetite for the world's resources is seemingly insatiable, but the appetite is not ultimately responsible for the environmental degradation that occurs to sate it: Third World governments sanction the use of these resources, deciding who has access to them and who does not. The degradation that results from this dispossession is thus closely linked to the global inequality in resources consumed and to local conflicts over control of these resources.

This has been the hidden dimension in El Salvador's civil war where, according to Howard Daugherty, coauthor of a Canadian government study of El Salvador's development options, "environmental degradation has resulted in extreme poverty, malnutrition, undernutrition, and dislocation of peoples — all of which has contributed to the current conflict."[12] With a high population density, virtually all of its forests denuded, and soil erosion affecting 77 percent of the country, El Salvador is a textbook example of too many people being squeezed into using too few resources. Five percent of the landowners have 70 percent of the arable land — most of it devoted to export markets — while the 80 percent who constitute the rural poor have only 14 percent.Eighty-six percent of farms have less than twelve acres, 50 percent less than two-and-a-half acres. To reduce the pressure for land redistribution, the landowners in Central America are strong advocates of birth control; they argue that the poor's rapid rate of reproduction is outstripping the region's ability to sustain them.

The Third World's poor sees things differently: far from straining the world's resources, they feel they are subsisting on only a portion of the fruits of its lands and seas, and paying a heavy price in the process. From their perspective, it is their elites, and we in the rich countries, who are not managing on our own inheritance of resources, but are depleting the stocks of others. And it is we who look lamely for excuses to explain this imbalance, and have struck upon the population explosion.

# 6

## *No wonder they're running out of food and fuel. Until they control their population it's a losing battle.*

"Where population growth has risen drastically, increasing numbers of people are harvesting crops as fast as the earth can produce them. At the same time, they are damaging the earth's ability to provide, and tropical forest is being lost at a frightening rate."
— From *News-Nouvelles*, the journal of the Planned Parenthood Federation of Canada, July, 1983.

"The good news is that what we can do with land is practically limitless. The bad news is that much of the land is in relatively few hands, and the prospect of land reform is not easy."
— Pierre Crosson, a researcher with the Washington-based Resources for the Future, in the *Toronto Star*, June 3, 1984.

EVERYONE HAS HEARD of the population explosion but few are aware that it is no more than the creation of computer-based projections of what the world in future would look like. As new information is coming in, those computer estimates are starting to fall.

In the last ten years alone, the annual growth in the world's population has shrunk from two percent to 1.7 percent. The most dramatic drop has occurred in China, where a policy of one child per family has been adopted, but the fertility rate has been dropping in most countries of the Third World, where population growth has been maintained because people are dying at a slower rate. The United Nations now predicts that the world's population will climb from our present 4.7 billion to a mere 6.1 billion by the year 2000 (down from some past estimates as high as 7.6 billion), and will stabilize at about ten billion around the year 2100.

The accuracy of these new global projections aside, their relevance to the ability of local populations to meet their local needs is rarely questioned. Problems associated with population tend to be felt locally, not globally, and when they arise they are dealt with locally. Even at the national level, the countries of the world are by no means unanimous in their resolve to lower population growth, or in the advisability of doing so.

While some, such as China, are going so far as to limit their populations by coercion, others are determined to increase the number of their citizens for economic and political reasons. The conventional wisdom that fewer mouths to feed means less spent on social services and more spent on productive investments seems to be dissipating. In the more affluent countries, higher populations are coming to be seen as essential to a vital economy.

In 1984, the European Commission and the European Parliament, fearing a shrinking slice of the world's economic pie, called for a halt to the decline in Europe's birth rate.[1] The common market countries of the European Economic Community are concerned that their population is likely to be halved as a proportion of the world's population in the second half of the 20th century, and could be halved again by 2025. France, which for several years has been encouraging births, holds the position that "cultures and civilizations rise and fall with the populations on which they are based .... this is the lesson of history." West Germany, whose population has been in decline since 1973, now offers tax incentives in a campaign to add 200,000 children a year to its population.

Eastern Europe also wants to reverse its declining population trend. East Germany is concerned because its population stopped growing in 1969. In Hungary, where the population has been on the decline since 1981, the government is encouraging larger families. In Romania, where the birth rate has dropped by 30 percent since 1975 and abortions outnumber live births, the legal age for marriage for girls has been lowered to 15 and people who are still single at 25 are taxed more heavily in an attempt to raise the population from 22 million to 25 million by 1990. The U.S.S.R. wants more workers to develop its vast north, and more people of Russian stock to counter the high birth rate of its Muslim population, who are making Russians a minority.

The popular view, promoted by bodies like the World Bank and the United Nations,[2] holds high population growth rates and high densities to blame for poverty, deforestation and other forms of environmental decay, and the famine they so often cause. In the words of Edouard Saouma, the director-general of the U.N.'s Food and Agriculture Organization, "many African countries, if they do not take action to encourage a drop in fertility rates, are speeding headlong to disaster."[3]

Yet the evidence to support these views does not seem to justify a link between population growth rates and environmental degradation or even a drop in personal wealth. Among Third World countries, the environment seems to be faring equally poorly in countries with relatively high population growth rates, like the Ivory Coast, and those with relatively low rates, like Haiti.[4] The absence of a link is even more striking when comparing population growth to poverty. Of the 30 poorest countries in the world, those that have improved the wealth of their inhabitants the most over the past two decades are China, Kenya, Malawi, Pakistan, and Sri Lanka: their population growth has averaged 2.7 percent per year. The worst economic performers, each with a fall in personal wealth, are Chad, Ghana, Madagascar, Niger, and Uganda. Population growth among this group is comparable: 2.6 percent per year.

Africa's ten richest countries have virtually the same population growth rate as the ten poorest. Kenya, which for the past two decades has averaged an extraordinarily high population growth rate of 3.6 percent per year and now has the world's highest, sustained an average increase in per capita wealth of 2.8 percent per year over those same 20 years.

High birth rates and young work forces may actually be a spur to economic development. They were features of Europe's economic boom in the last century and of Japan's and the Far East's in this one. According to the Population Research Institute in Japan's Nihon University, because fertility rates have been dropping so severely, Japan's economic heyday may be drawing to a close.[5] The Institute's theories, complete with its own computer models, have surprising breadth supporting its contention that population growth is a key to prosperity: at the United Nations' first population conference in Bucharest in 1974, the advocates of population growth were Marxists; a decade later, at the

U.N.'s second population conference in Mexico City, the U.S. government under the Reagan administration concurred with the view that people are not the problem.

The most fundamental of arguments against the population bomb — that the earth's carrying capacity can simply not support the additional billions to come — also seems to be wearing thin. Although the Global 2000 Report to the President,[6] commissioned by President Carter, concludes that total world farmland will increase by only four percent by the end of the century because "most good land is already being cultivated," and the computer projections of the last decade, published in the bestseller, *Limits to Growth*,[7] assumes that the potential for increasing food production is small, other studies, and recent history, undermine their findings.

Population growth rates were at a peak in past decades but world food production surpassed them nevertheless, rising by 75 percent from 1960 to 1980 while population rose by 48 percent. According to the Food and Agriculture Organization, the remaining potential in the decades ahead is great: only one half of the world's savannas, grasslands, and other potentially arable land is under cultivation today. "Many African and Latin countries still have relatively ample land resources," it says, while in Asia "great scope exists for increased production through irrigation and multicropping."[8]

Using current Western farming methods, the FAO believes the world could produce enough food for up to 33 billion people, seven times the present population. Using less sophisticated farming methods, 15 billion could be fed and even if the whole world relied on traditional farming methods, using no fertilizers or pesticides, no soil conservation methods and traditional seeds, the present world population could still be comfortably fed. In Africa, some desert countries, like Ethiopia, Niger, and Mauritania, may be short of land to feed their people but in others, including Angola, the Ivory Coast, Zaire, and Zambia, the people could, using current methods, feed five times their number if they wanted to maximize the food they produced. The Congo could feed 20 times its population, Gabon 100 times. Overall, Africa could, with traditional methods, feed 2.7 times its current population.

The certainty of global resource shortages caused by population explosions no longer seems so certain. Local shortages, in contrast, are always developing and in response to them people are always moving to more affluent areas, or adapting their agricultural methods, or developing new industries, or adjusting in some other way, such as by varying the size of their families. Because of their adjustments, severe local shortages normally don't occur abruptly, except in the case of natural disasters like drought and unnatural ones such as those that forcibly dispossess people of their land. Areas can become poor, and these same areas often become depopulated — either through migration or birth control — as they become unable to sustain their residents. Some families see their members leave to seek a better life elsewhere; some contract in size when fewer children allow each member a larger share of the family income.

But rich areas like the Western countries, where families often view more than one or two children as luxuries or inconveniences, may react as the poor areas do and also decrease their population.

In the same way that families in either rich or poor countries decrease in size when it suits their particular circumstances, they may increase in size when those circumstances change: affluent areas sometimes want to increase their populations to become more affluent, and poor areas sometimes want more children to become less poor.

In India's rural areas, children join the labor force when they are as young as six years and help in tending livestock, carrying water, and collecting fuelwood, dung, and other forms of energy. Unlike Western children, who are often viewed as economic burdens, Third World children are quickly converted from burdens to assets, and as long as there is more work to be done, there is an incentive to produce more children. Because women are the workhorses in the Third World household, expending 53 percent of human energy compared to 31 percent for men and 16 percent for children, they stand most to gain from additional offspring, which offsets the burden of bearing them.[9]

Children, because they plant crops and collect firewood, often insure that families in the Third World don't run out of food and fuel. Two or three children are generally considered necessary for an Indian household's survival, but in regions that have suffered from policies that have led to extreme environmental degradation, the number will often be higher.[10]

In parts of India where overexploitation has led to deforestation, one person in a family of five must work full-time finding fuel. In Bara in the Sudan, where a decade ago fuelwood could be found 15 minutes from the village, a one-to-two hour's walk is now required. In Nepal, journeys to gather firewood and fodder in the Himalayan foothills now take a whole day, compared to an hour or two a generation ago. In central Tanzania, it takes the equivalent of one person working five days a week to gather a week's fuelwood for the family, in the African Sahel it takes the equivalent of three hours a day, in Niger four hours a day, and in the

Gambia from noon to nightfall just to gather an evening's supply.

Over the course of years, decades, and generations, these people have been changing with the changing conditions imposed on them, making the best of their available options, only one of which is altering their population. Some are better off despite these hardships, some worse off, but all are managing as well as can reasonably be expected, given the enormity of the problems they face.

When families do alter their size, they do not do so in isolation, but accommodate in their decisions a host of volatile social and economic conditions that reflect their personal circumstances and that of their community. This dynamic complex of factors which determines population growth cannot be modeled by any computer or coordinated by any central body; yet, because their result — the population growth itself — can be quantified, planned for, and, presumably controlled centrally, there have been attempts to do so.

This tendency is reinforced by a commonly held belief that a measure of outside discipline is desirable because people always have a tendency to exploit the environment for short-term gain, and nowhere is this better shown, the theory goes, than in communally held lands, where the inherent inability of human beings to restrain their greed makes the plunder of these common lands inevitable.

# 7

## *The tragedy of deforestation is the tragedy of the commons*

"What does a high birth rate do to a country? .... It leads to overuse and damaging of agricultural land and deforestation; in Gambia and Tanzania, population growth has made wood so scarce that each household spends 250 to 300 worker-days a year gathering wood."
— "The fertility battle," editorial in the *Globe and Mail*, July 21, 1984.

"This forest is our mother's home, we will protect it with all our might."
— The chant of the women of the Chipko movement in India's Himalayas when protecting their communal forests from commercial loggers.

THE THEORY OF THE Tragedy of the Commons, popularized by Garrett Hardin's classic essay of 1968, blames the depletion of the world's finite resources on the self-interest of individuals.[1] Using the example of ranchers who graze their cattle on community pastureland, he describes how, up to a certain point, the addition of more cows by any rancher does not affect the amount of grass other ranchers' cows can eat. But beyond the point at which there is just enough for every cow to eat its fill, if any rancher adds just one more cow all the cows will end up slightly less plump.

The owner of the additional cow is nevertheless better off because he keeps all of the profits to be made from his additional cow. It is always in his self-interest to increase his use of the commons although that use comes at the expense of all the other ranchers. When every rancher acts this way, a vicious cycle is set off whereby each new cow added contributes to a loss for all. In the end everyone becomes impoverished because the common resource has not been wisely managed, but left to the selfish devices of individuals.

"Therein is the tragedy," Hardin concludes. "Each man is locked into a system that compels him to increase his herd without limit — in a world that is limited. Ruin is the destination toward which all men rush, each pursuing his own best interest in a society that believes in the freedom of the commons. Freedom in the commons brings ruin to all."

Using Hardin's logic, development experts have blamed Third World peasants for overexploiting their forests. They see forests so denuded that villagers have to walk further and further from their homes each year in search of fuelwood,[2] and they attribute this ruin to the relentlessly increasing populations who disregard the needs of the common forests to satisfy their individual needs.

But this explanation of the cause and effect of deforestation ignores the communities that have sustainably maintained their common forests over many generations. In Guatemala, the Indians of Totonicapan have kept communal forests intact for four centuries because they recognized the economic value of their white pines, the mainstay of their furniture industry since the 1500s.[3] In Totonicapan, a state in western Guatemala, each city and town that maintains a communal forest is responsible for supervising its use and for deciding which uses best serve the common interests of the community.

The effect has been to keep the forests intact. Because so many members of each community depend on the income generated from woodcutting and carpentry, they need little other incentive to see that no one within their community takes from the forest more than his share, and no one from without infringes on their property rights. Their successful self-regulation has been aided by a pride in their independence from outside influence and control, and by an absence of anonymity: people generally recognize each other on sight (if not individually at least by family or village), creating a mutual sense of community which contributes to the respect for the forest boundaries.

The success that the Indians of Totonicapan have had in managing their "commons" has been paralleled by other communities in other Third World countries. Throughout pre-colonial India, communal village woodlots, located in village commons or along roadsides, were prevalent. These mini-forests provided a sustainable supply of fuel, fodder, fruit, oil, medicine, and timber for the community while maintaining the soil's fertility, preventing its erosion, and conserving underground and surface water. The presence of private woodlots serving private purposes nearby did not prevent the coexistence of the communal woodlots, whose use was guided by community norms.[4] But beginning in the nineteenth century, when the British Raj reserved large tracts of communal forests for commercial purposes, the communal system broke down. Rural populations who lost control over their forests became alienated from them; others, who saw how easily the same fate could befall them, became insecure in their rights. In India, communal forests were not threatened until these outside claims — first by the colonial government, later by the national government — overrode the village's traditional property rights. The subsequent decline of community participation soon led to disastrous outcomes, with formerly well managed community forests turned into unmanaged commons. The village's communal ownership system, under which the individual was accountable to the community, was replaced by the state's ownership, which made the individual accountable to a distant and alien power.

The forests reserved for the state, ironically, fared no better, dwindling through inefficient and misguided commercial overexploitation.[5] This decline, which began in 1865, was followed by a steady procession of legislation and regulations that have transferred community owned forest land to the state and to government-run forest development corporations.

Under proposed new legislation in India, "any land whatsoever .... which the State government declares to be a forest" becomes state property and anyone who is found "gathering forest produce," which includes grass, flowers, leaves and branches, is punishable by up to three years imprisonment and a fine of 5,000 rupees, or about $500. Here the Indian government has gone one step further: to protect the Hardin-type commons from the local population that still depends on it, the government intends to outlaw the population's traditional uses.[6] Access to the forest, which had been limited to the community and the industries it relied upon, was denied them and opened up by state sanction to far-flung consumers, an expansion devoid of accountability which creates Hardin's tragic "commons".

Tragic commons elsewhere were created under similar circumstances, and through a similar process. In Kenya, the takeover of communal forests and tribal lands by the colonial government's national Forest Department disrupted the tribes' customary rights, their rules of access, their influence, and their authority over the use of their forests.[7]

HARDIN'S EQUATION FOR DISASTER – too many people trying to use the same amount of land – focussed exclusively on the imbalance caused by the first half of that equation, population growth leading to overexploitation, forgetting that the imbalance can just as easily occur by tampering with the second half by reducing the amount of land.

This is the case in Central America every time a communal forest is allocated by government deed to private cattle-ranching interests, and in South-East Asia every time a communal forest is signed over to a Japanese logging company. Yet it is not the commercial interests that are pointed to for upsetting the balance but the people. Organizations like the United Nations' Food and Agriculture Organization do not even mention who has upset the status quo when they blame the rural inhabitants for "indiscriminate firewood collection, excessive lopping of trees and overgrazing" which damages their forests "sometimes beyond repair."[8] In effect, instead of questioning the legitimacy of the outside intervention which has such devastating effects, they are blaming the victims of decisions taken by forces outside their control.

For these outside forces to prevail, they must somehow acquire pre-eminent control over a community's property rights. But if a community can protect its traditional property rights, it may be able to manage its resources sustainably even when the outside forces seem far more menacing.[9]

Totonicapan did, under conditions of extreme hardship. During its conquest by the Spanish the land became unable to support its population, which dropped to 30,000 or 40,000 — less than half its population before the colonial period, and less than one quarter of its present population of 167,000. The difference in the land's carrying capacity stemmed primarily from one requirement of the Spaniards: the payment of a tax in the form of wool. Because large areas of land were required for sheep pasture, land which had previously yielded food for the local population was plowed under to yield wool for outsiders instead. Even worse, the sheep's overgrazing led to extreme soil erosion, which today still plagues half of Totonicapan's land area. As the sheep population increased during the Spaniards' 200-year stay in Totonicapan, the Indian population dropped.

To meet its food needs, the Indians began to import food from neighboring regions. In exchange for the food, cottage industries, most of them based on the Indian's pine forests, sprang up. Today, Totonicapan has a four-century old furniture industry and its community of carpenters recognize well the economic value of the white pine forests. While neighboring regions have lost more than 60 percent of their forest over roughly the same period, Totonicapan's forests have remained stable despite a population increase of over 80 percent.[10]

Hardin's fear, that everyone is locked into a ruinous cycle, may be well founded when individuals are unrestrained in pursuing their "own best interest" in a society that tolerates the plundering of its commons. But the self-interest and unaccountability described in Hardin's model is not the rule. In communities where those who depend on a resource also control it, social systems that regulate their take from the land have evolved. Despite the ability to plunder a common good, despite population growth, and sometimes even despite external pressures, these societies have maintained an equilibrium between their demands on their resources and their resource's ability to satisfy their demands precisely because they have managed to keep their commons.

But protecting the commons, especially when the commons comes in the form of the air we breathe or the water we drink — commodities generally devoid of commercial worth — is not a universally recognized value. To many, other priorities come first.

# 8

## *The Third World can't afford to worry about protecting its environment when it has more important things to worry about – like feeding its billions.*

"We cannot afford ecological luxury."
– The view of Vasudevan Nair, Premier of India's Kerala State, about the flooding of the Silent Valley and its 50-million-year-old biological heritage, quoted in *The State of India's Environment*.

"But the plant genetic diversity is an immense economic resource that the state can ill afford to lose. Genes from the wild plants, which have undergone a fantastic natural selection process, can be cross-bred in cultivated crops to incorporate disease resistance and drought endurance characteristics."
– From *The State of India's Environment*

NO SOCIETY, WHETHER in the rich industrialized West or in the poor Third World, can afford to allow its environment to degrade because the ultimate profitability of its economy depends on the health of the physical environment. Yet many leaders around the world still see economic development as a zero-sum game in which improved living standards can only be achieved at the expense of the environment.

Indira Gandhi at the 1972 *United Nations Conference on the Human Environment in Stockholm*, was loudly endorsed for describing "poverty [as] the worst form of pollution." More recently, a former Prime Minister of Nepal lamented the slow development of his country with the similar sentiment that "[we] could do with a little industrial smog."[1]

The belief that environmental degradation is a sign of progress, that environmental protection is better tackled after a country builds an industrial base which generates wealth, prevails, even in some Western countries, where the belief is still often held dear.

Canada in 1982 saw a battle over an electricity export project that would have increased coal burning, and so acid-gas emissions. The province of Ontario wanted to build an underwater cable across Lake Erie to link the Ontario electricity grid to U.S. markets — a link that it thought necessary to develop Ontario's electricity system.[2] Because of the great damage this project could cause to the environment — acidified lakes, damage to forests and croplands, and lung disease in humans — the federal government insisted on the installation of pollution-abatement equipment. Ontario refused because the costs of this equipment would have made its project uneconomical. As far as the province was concerned, environmental protection was a luxury it could not afford.[3]

Nevertheless, the realization that environmental protection is consistent with economic prosperity is taking hold. Since the 1972 United Nations Conference and the 1973 OPEC oil crisis, the West's industrial leaders have generally found that the government's strict environmental guidelines have not hurt their profits, as they had expected, but have helped them. Emissions from petrochemical plants have been cut back to one-five-hundredth of what had been permitted a decade ago through cleaner techniques which conserve resources, and energy savings of 80 percent in new office buildings have become routine.[4]

Conservation and pollution abatement can be good economics, not just for individual businesses or households but for the economy as a whole. The assumption that wealth and environmental decay can coexist or that environmental degradation is a necessary by-product of wealth is slowly changing as evidence shows that development without regard for the environment is akin to killing the goose that lays the golden egg.

Some of the best illustrations of how neglect of the environment backfires are found in schemes to develop hydropower and forestry resources.

India's Planning Commission, discouraged by the enormous environmental and social costs that resulted from two decades of dam building, started the third by beginning a review of its existing hydro dams. This review probably represents the first effort by a Third World country to take a fresh look at the costs and benefits of large dams. With the advantage of hindsight, the Planning Commission found that some of the dams would never have been built had all the costs been included in the original analysis. Among the costs usually overlooked in the original feasibility studies are the costs of resettling people; the environmental costs of soil erosion, landslides, and flooding that followed the deforestation of the catchment areas; and the human and property costs of earthquakes that occurred in formerly inactive seismic areas. In one of the reexamined projects, the Bhima project in the state of Maharashtra, the costs of the project turned out to be more than twice its benefits.[5]

India's forestry industry has yet to undergo a review similar to the one the dam builders are receiving, but it appears they will need to learn the same lessons about the need to protect the environment.

In the southern part of the Indian State of Bihar, the State Forest Development Corporation decided in 1977 to "upgrade" its mixed forests by replacing them with a monoculture of teak, which it plans to export. The existing forests which would have to go to make room for the teak include those of the sal tree, which the forests' tribal population regards as sacred and which serves a wide number of local needs. The sal's leaves are used for making platters and cups, the soft kernel of its fruit is used to make a sweet paste, and the oil from its seeds is used for cooking. The sal also supports a wide range of birds and animals that will not adapt themselves to a teak forest.[6]

Teak not only lacks these properties but, like the eucalyptus, it does not hold the soil well. It will neither protect the land from the ravages of deforestation nor provide the local population with the essentials of life.

Monocultures of pine, another species which can seriously degrade soil by acidifying it and reducing its capacity to hold water, have also been replacing sal forests, such as those of Madhya Pradesh state in central India, where the World Bank has funded a pine plantation and paper mill project.[7]

In the state of Tamil Nadu, the Bombay Natural History Society, an Indian research body, has come to conclusions about bamboo forests similar to those the Indian Planning Commission arrived at for hydro dams. Its analysis found that

> the reduction in bamboo stocks in the forest in Tamil Nadu has taken us one step nearer to the point when deforestation will be reducing large tracts of land in the hills to near-desert conditions and in the process inflicting devastation on down-stream areas in the form of growing floods as well as increasing aridity and drought.[8]

The Society further pointed out that six-and-a-half billion tons of soil a year, along with as many tons of valuable plant nutrients, are already washed away from the Himalayan belt alone. "The plant nutrients thus lost each year amount to more than the total consumption of chemical fertilizer in the country today."[9]

This huge loss in agricultural assets can be measured against the priority India otherwise places on improving agricultural output — no less than 40 percent of all federal subsidies go toward food and artificial fertilizers.[10]

Like India, other countries will learn their lesson only after great damage has been done.

In Brazil, Electronorte, a giant utility, and the builders of Tucurui, the largest hydro dam ever undertaken in a tropical forest, believes that in the Amazon "any dam is economic, most of all if you consider that the land is free. The only price is the environmental one."[11] The utility's accountants may be surprised to discover how high the environmental cost can be: very few dams have been built in tropical rain forests anywhere in the world, and their history has been an unhappy one. Lake Brokopondo in the former Dutch colony of Surinam, the first tropical dam of any size, flooded 600 square miles of virgin rain forest to create its reservoir. As the vegetation decomposed it acidified the water to the point that it corroded the dam's expensive cooling system. (The hydrogen sulphide which was produced also caused a stink so strong it forced workers at the dam to wear gas masks and was smelled several miles downwind.) Meanwhile water hyacinth, a weed which until then had been rare in Surinam, started to thrive on the decaying trees and spread over the lake surface, impeding navigation and tangling machinery. Within a year, an eight-square-mile carpet of water hyacinth was floating on Lake Brokopondo and by the following year almost half the reservoir was covered by the weed. Another weed, a floating fern, blanketed another 25 square miles.[12]

At the newest dam in the Amazon basin, the Curua Una near Santarem, decomposition and waterweeds led to complaints of sulphurous smell for months after the uncleared reservoir began filling. After the smells evaporated other troubles arose. Acidic water corroded the steel casings of the dam's turbines and water hyacinth and sedge, another weed, covered half the reservoir.

Because water hyacinth is unpalatable and even toxic to most fish, many of them died. Water hyacinth also absorbed the lake's available nutrients and blocked the sun's rays from penetrating to the depths of the lake, killing the plants and fish that depended on them. At Jupia, a Brazilian dam on the Parana River outside the Amazon region, the sheer weight of the water hyacinth growing on the lake's surface has snapped steel cables. Specially designed filters intended to protect the turbines from water weeds have been so clogged that the dam has had to be shut down from time to time.[13]

To add to the chaos, because water hyacinths and other weeds greatly increase the effective surface area of the reservoir or lake, losses of water through evaporation can rise by up to six times the normal rate.[14] This phenomenon, known as evapotranspiration, jeopardizes the capacity of reservoirs and dams to generate electricity or irrigate surrounding farmland.

Deforestation of the surrounding uplands also decreases the volume of the reservoir because of the topsoil that runs off. Brazil loses more soil to erosion than any other country, with 6,500 billion cubic yards, an average of eight tons per acre of agricultural soil, carried off the land annually.[15]

If one of Brazil's multi-million dollar dams is destroyed by siltation caused by deforestation, it will not be the first time that environmental degradation ruined the profitability of a Brazilian hydro project. In the watershed of the Rio Alta Pardo in Brazil, soil erosion led to such severe runoff that in 1977 two dams on the river were completely destroyed.[16]

But it is in Sri Lanka where neglect of the Mahaweli River watershed may end in human tragedies on a different scale. Having committed over $2 billion to construct four dams and open up 320,000 acres of rain forest and marginal scrub lands to agriculture, the giant river has been left with only eight percent of its watershed forested. Fears are looming large that, with over 100 inches of rain a year and so few trees to anchor the hillsides, landslides could break one of the dams and drown the 100,000 inhabitants of Gampola and Kandy.[17] "PhD students will flock to Sri Lanka in a few years' time and write learned theses on the inappropriateness of high technology aid for poor countries," predicts a Sri Lankan lawyer, Gamini Iriyagolle, a specialist on the Mahaweli program.[18] "It will destroy our civilization within 15 years."

The failure to recognize the cost of ignoring the environment is widespread: disasters from neglect of the environment are commonplace in countries around the world, as are cavalier attitudes toward the environment. Until we learn that environmental protection is not a luxury but a necessity, efforts to create wealth will be undermined.

Calamities like landslides are often dubbed "natural disasters" yet their origins can be entirely man-made. This is the case with landslides, and it is the case with floods.

# 9

## *Floods are an act of God*

"Climatic changes precipitated by *El Niño* current off the west coast of South America in late 1982 and early 1983 created severe drought in the dry plateau and valleys of Bolivia and produced floods in lowland areas."
— From the 1983 Annual Report of the Inter-American Development Bank.

"It is largely man's environmental mismanagement that makes worldwide hazards out of droughts, famine, floods, hurricanes, and earthquakes."
— Jon Tinker, Director of Earthscan, quoted in the *Christian Science Monitor*, Aug. 25, 1984.

WITH THE EXCEPTION of Noah's flood, and other cataclysms, floods generally do not come down upon us from on high but are the work of mortals who know not, or care not, what they do. Floods are less the result of an overabundance of rainfall than of the inability of the soil to absorb rain. Unabsorbed, it quickly runs off into rivers, swelling them to the point of flooding, even under normal rainfall.[1]

Nothing helps soil absorb water better than trees. Tropical forests act like sponges, soaking up rainfall before releasing it slowly and steadily to streams and rivers. Just 6,000 acres of forest, for instance, can hold as much water as a 100 million cubic yard reservoir.

South America's tropical forests recycle as much as 75 percent of their rainfall back to the atmosphere:[2] approximately one quarter of the Amazon's rainfall is returned to the atmosphere from raindrops that evaporate from the leaves of trees and other vegetation and as much as one half is returned by transpiration, a process in which moisture is absorbed by tree roots from the soil and carried by the plants' veins back up to the leaves and exuded through their pores. Only the remaining one quarter of the original rainfall actually leaves the region in the form of streams or rivers.

The leaves of the trees do double-duty, both breaking the fall of raindrops so that they reach the ground as a fine spray and channeling them into a trickle down the tree, laden with nutrients from the leaves and bark. Without a heavy mass of vegetation to break the fall of rain, water runoff greatly increases because the rate at which water seeps into the soil is considerably lower.

Removing trees, especially those lining rivers or their tributaries, leads to greater runoff, rising levels of streams, and flooding of lowland areas. To make matters worse, when a forest is cleared, losing its net of tree roots which holds its topsoil in place, the topsoil is carried by the water runoff into the rivers, where much of it settles on the river bottom. This reduces the volume of water the river can hold, and also increases the likelihood of floods.

In the last few years, the bed of the Ganga River in India has risen by one-and-a-half feet, and the beds of the Terai rivers have been rising at the rate of six to twelve inches per year.[3]

In man-made attempts to control flooding, dams have been built to collect the run-off. But topsoil carried by the river from the surrounding lands into the dams' reservoir have drastically reduced their capacity to hold water, rendering them incapable of absorbing heavy rains. To prevent dams from bursting, panic releases sometimes occur, leading to destructive flash floods in the valleys downstream. India's Punjab region experienced one such disaster in 1978 when 65,000 people were left homeless.[4]

The amount of land susceptible to flooding appears to be increasing. In India, according to the National Commission on Floods, the total area subject to periodic floods has swelled from 50 million acres in 1971 to 100 million acres in 1981. This doubling in one decade occurred despite government programs designed to flood-proof 20 million acres.[5]

The findings of the Commission only confirmed what the local people in those areas already knew. Before the denudation of their forests, these disastrous floods were unknown to them; after the deforestation, they became commonplace. In one year, 1978, 55 out of 56 districts in the state of Uttar Pradesh were affected by floods. That year India suffered from the worst flooding in its history: two days of rainfall left 66,000 villages inundated, more than 2,000 people drowned, and 40,000 cattle swept away. Two states, West Bengal and Uttar Pradesh, lost a total of $750 million in crops.[6]

Deforestation is credited with causing floods elsewhere as well: in the Philippines' Davao Del Norte Province, where the area's civil defense director admits "if we have two or three days of continuous rain, it will flood every time;" in the basin of the Nepalese rivers, where the acreage flooded has increased four times in the past 25 years; in Thailand, where flooding now afflicts some 1,000 villages; and in China, where the banks of the Yangtze overflowed in 1980 in one of the worst floods in Chinese history, affecting ten million people in Szechwan province and destroying hundreds of million of dollars worth of property.[7]

China considers the large floods in Szechwan and other parts of the country to be grave warnings of worse natural calamities to come if no measures are taken to check ecological imbalances. The government has launched a nationwide tree-planting campaign, requiring all able-bodied people over the age of eleven to plant three to five trees a year. In this massive attempt to avert man-made floods, China's government has also imposed a strict ban on indiscriminate tree felling, outlawed the cutting of trees near water sources, and directed peasants to plant trees instead of crops on steep hillsides to help curb erosion. Further measures taken by the Chinese include planting tree belts to function as dikes, building more reservoirs, and dredging and diverting rivers. According to Professor Guan Junwei, an expert in soil conservation, the Chinese have developed innovative methods as well, such as the construction of fishponds near cropland which serve to detain flood water and prevent soil erosion.[8] The general thrust of China's approach is to avoid major engineering works like dams, embankments, and dredging in favor of forest conservation and watershed management.

But China is an exception. Most countries swallow their fears and hope they'll avoid calamities on the scale that China experienced. In Sri Lanka, the government has been warned that erosion, landslides, and flooding could damage the massive Mahaweli series of hydroelectric and irrigation dams that it has staked so much of Sri Lanka's future on,[9] yet reforestation and water management have been the poor sisters of the project. With the costs of the project almost doubling, the government has run out of the funds needed to replant the hillsides, spending only one quarter of one percent of the necessary amount to date.

The Mahaweli project is the world's largest foreign aid project, involving a facelift to one third of its land mass and the relocation of ten percent of its population. To undertake this project required the combined support of many of the world's major aid agencies: the World Bank, the Asian Development Bank, the European Economic Community, and the aid agencies of Great Britain, Canada, West Germany, Sweden, Japan, and Kuwait. Neither they, nor the Sri Lankan government, have to look far to discover the consequences of ignoring the needs of the environment: neighboring India and nearby China provide chilling testimonials. Yet, almost inexplicably, no lessons seem to have been learned.

# 10

## *Development experts have learned a lot from the mistakes they have made in the past*

"In the bad old days, which were not so long ago, an army loudspeaker truck would go through the affected villages a couple of weeks before the reservoir waters reached them and say 'listen fellas, you've got two weeks to hop it, goodbye.' And in a week's time, if they hadn't gone, there might be coercion."
— The World Bank's Robert Goodland illustrates how unaccountable development projects were in the past.

"All I can tell you is that there is a dam funded by the World Bank and a smelter owned by Kaiser. Everything else is confidential."
— Tobias Asser, a World Bank lawyer, refuses to be interviewed in the *Multinational Monitor* about a World Bank project.

"THINGS HAVE IMPROVED GREATLY over the old days," explained World Bank ecologist Robert Goodland at a 1983 conference on *Hydroelectric Projects and Native Peoples*.[1]

"Very thorough surveys of the people to be affected are undertaken before any construction is started. The rule now is that the people must be better off and certainly no worse off after being relocated. This is a sign, I think, that we are moving in the right direction."

Similar pledges to move "in the right direction" were also made in February 1980, when ten international development organizations signed a joint *Declaration of Environmental Policies and Procedures Relating to Economic Development*. In so doing, they undertook to mend their ways and institute environmental protection procedures in their programs.[2]

Unfortunately, there has not been as much progress as well-wishing by Goodland and the signatories to the Declaration: although aid experts now know the extent of the havoc their projects have wreaked in the past, they are no more obliged today to consider social and environmental factors when deciding which projects to fund. In fact, little of substance has changed since the 1950s, when projects such as Ghana's Akosombo Dam were undertaken. In those heady days of development, the stated policy — to make "no one worse off"[3] — was identical to the current expressions of faith.

While surveys of the people to be affected by a project are more likely to be conducted today than they were a quarter century ago, their results are almost never used to determine whether a project proceeds, even when the surveys are "very thorough". For the most part, the surveys appear to be used for window-dressing. According to one World Bank consultant, David Price, the World Bank is "much more concerned with images than with the welfare of the native minorities."[4]

Hired as a consultant in 1980, Price was asked to

evaluate how well the Brazilian government could safeguard the rights of 8,000 Indians who would be affected by a World Bank-backed project,[5] even though the World Bank had already given the Brazilian government carte blanche to treat the Indians as they chose. Price's findings, which were damning of the Brazilian government, were not published and circulation of his final report was restricted. In the World Bank's official internal report, his findings and recommendations were altered so seriously that he complained in a letter to the World Bank President that the document "systematically distorts material that I furnished so as to make it support conclusions radically opposed to my own."[6]

In practice, surveys to protect those who will be affected by a foreign aid project are conducted by the Third World government, not by the aid agency whose prime responsibility is the financing of the project. Yet the Third World government, as the proponent of the project, cannot be expected to represent fairly the views of those citizens who oppose it.

Environmental assessments, although they generally fall under the aid agency's purview, are also paper exercises. Full assessments rarely occur; more often aid officials simply run their projects through a short checklist of potential environmental problems. The officials are almost never obliged to obtain independent environmental assessments, nor do the assessments have to meet any standards. Environmental assessments, like the surveys taken of the people who may be forced off their land, almost never determine whether a project proceeds or not.[7]

A study commissioned by the European Economic Community in 1983[8] found that the multilateral development banks which signed the 1980 Declaration have done little to change their policies. John Horberry, the author of the study of environmental procedures, found "little evidence of the application of existing guidelines." In fact, "some agencies never put some guidelines into operation because their function is to improve public relations." In a statement to 1984 U.S. Congressional hearings, Horberry summarized his findings unequivocally:

> Looking at the performance of multilaterals in general, most have the appearance of responding to environmental and natural resource management problems, but few have really effective policies and procedures. Despite statements of policy, none have environmental staff or resources commensurate with the objectives of the Declaration. None have environmental procedures that project staff are required to follow. None have placed environmental analysis at the core of project planning and appraisal.[9]

The Inter-American Development Bank, which in 1982 approved 79 loans averaging $34.7 million, has no environmental office and only one environmental staff member. A series of environmental checklists is available to the staff although it is not required to apply them. Despite this, a 1983 publication from this bank claimed that it had "stressed systematic consideration for proper management of the environment, incorporating it as an integral part in planning the different projects."[10]

Claims like this leave the Natural Resources Defense Council, a non-profit legal group attempting to improve the accountability of international development institutions, in disbelief:

> Incredibly, some of the projects cited in the IDB environmental progress report are internationally notorious examples of .... environmental disasters. One of these, the Sinu River Development Project in Colombia, will involve the construction of the country's largest dam. The dam will create three reservoirs — inundating 173,000 acres of tropical forest and displacing 2,000 Indians and thousands of peasants — and will permanently alter the ecological and sociological balance of the entire region.[11]

Even the World Bank, which has the most sophisticated and long-lived environmental review procedures of any development bank, has only five full-time professionals employed in its Office of Environmental Affairs out of a total of 5,250 employees. On these five people rests the impossible task of monitoring hundreds of ongoing projects and examining the approximately 300 new projects that are approved each year.

"So many projects are going on in developing countries," Goodland acknowledged, "that it is impossible for international financiers to take careful cognizance of everything."[12]

With so few staff and so many projects with enormous and unknown environmental side-effects, it is no wonder that the World Bank hasn't required full environmental assessments to be carried out early enough in the selection process to question a project's feasibility. As told by the NRDC's Bruce Rich to a U.S. congressional hearing, "the Bank's sole mandatory environmental procedures call for the review of projects long after they have been chosen and designed, and just before the initiation of loan negotiations."[13]

The performance of the aid agencies of Western governments is not much better. Apart from the U.S. Agency for International Development, these bilateral aid agencies are no more bound than their multilateral counterparts to count environmental costs in the feasibility formulas that determine whether a project proceeds or not. AID is unique among both bilateral and multilateral aid agencies in having to follow a set of legally binding procedures to insure that environmental factors will influence projects. The national aid agencies of Canada, West Germany, the Netherlands, Sweden, and the U.K., according to the International Institute for Environment and Development, a research body funded by the U.N. and various aid agencies, all lack these procedures.[14]

But even the U.S. procedures fall far short of protecting the environment, or of guaranteeing that the rights of people who face the expropriation of their lands will be respected. Like the other Western aid agencies, AID does not require that public hearings be held in Third World countries. In effect, the assessments are conducted behind closed doors, without a guarantee of public input, and without public review of the conclusions. The failure to open foreign aid projects to public scrutiny constitutes the most serious mistake that aid experts have made in the past and the one they have learned the least from. Because of the shroud of secrecy under which decisions are made the decision, the decision-making process, and ultimately the development process itself are poisoned.

The failure of Western governments to require that public hearings be held for their foreign aid projects stands alone: domestically, public hearings are ordinarily required for all aspects of projects, on all manner of subjects, whenever taxpayers' money is spent. The right to these hearings, though sometimes hard won, has had salutary results. In

Canada, for example, two extensive reviews of large development projects in the last decade — the Mackenzie Valley pipeline in the Arctic, which would have had a dramatic and direct impact on native populations, and Ontario Hydro's electricity expansion program, which affected a much larger population in less dramatic ways — helped to make better, if not perfect, decisions.[15] Despite claims by champions of the projects that they were needed too urgently to invest years in public hearings, the time was taken, generating a wealth of information and a wealth of views about the way the projects would affect Canadians' lifestyles and their economy. The information from each hearing provided a better base from which to make decisions, and the exercise itself made the decision-making process more equitable and, as a result, more legitimate.

When such a process is absent, as it is with virtually all foreign aid projects, the disruption can be immense, and the opposition can be widespread. Sri Lanka's giant Mahaweli project is one of the chief contributors to the sectarian violence between the majority Sinhalese and the minority Tamils. The Tamils view the giant scheme, which will ultimately relocate one-and-a-half million people, as an attempt by the Sinhalese to outnumber them in their own lands as a prelude to destroying their culture.[16]

In Haiti, a foreign aid project is not merely a contributor to a problem but the problem itself. There the residents of the country's richest agricultural area first learned they would be losing their homes and farms from the foreign surveyor who came to their valley, sparking opposition that ultimately included the 7,000 small farmers and tenant farmers who would be directly affected, farmers from neighboring communities, leaders of the Catholic church, human rights activists, and rural development workers.

To oppose the project — two hydroelectric dams which would flood their lands — the peasants first sent an appeal to the Inter-American Development Bank, the foreign-aid agency funding the preliminary work. The IDB, which receives its funds from the foreign aid budgets of the U.S., Canada, and other Western governments, responded with assurances that everyone who would be worse off as a result of the dam would be identified in its study and appropriate measures would be taken to compensate those affected. But when asked by the peasants if they could review this study, the bank officials responded that the IDB "finances this study at the request of the Haitian government, and we suggest you contact the concerned government authorities for further details."[17] The authorities happen to be the government of "Baby Doc" Duvalier, widely recognized as one of the most repressive regimes in the world.

A church-based human rights group in France, meanwhile, had commissioned a study of the impact of the proposed Haitian dams to obtain the information the Haitian government and IDB officials would not release. This independent study, which was conducted by a team of economists, sociologists, and agronomists, is highly detailed, describing, crop-by-crop, the effect of these dams on Haiti's food production, estimating the impact on Haiti's level of unemployment, and describing the overall consequences of the dams for the local population.[18]

It concluded that the dam would be ill-advised. Thousands of small farmers and tenant farmers would lose their livelihood and be forced into the slums of Port-au-Prince, the capital city, where the unemployment rate was an estimated 50 percent. Haiti's ability to feed itself would deteriorate, with the food supply of between 30,000 and 60,000 Haitians being wiped out, forcing the country to become more dependent on food imports. Moreover, the value of the output from the hydroelectric dams would be 40 percent less than the value of the current agricultural output of the land.

Despite the gravity of the study's findings, the IDB refused to comment on its conclusions. An analysis of the dam's environmental and social aspects would be conducted, a bank official disclosed, but not "in a sentimental way".[19] Canada's own foreign aid agency, CIDA, which had financed an earlier study identifying the areas to be flooded and which is responsible for Canadian participation in the IDB,[20] also refused comment.

The peasants in Haiti hadn't needed the study to recognize their predicament. With a growing desperation, 8,500 people from the region had mustered the courage to sign a petition in January 1982 protesting the dam. To circumvent Haiti's secret police, the petition was circulated by the Catholic church through all of the country's church parishes, its text was read aloud in all the church services, it was then broadcast over a church-sponsored radio station, and published in two Haitian periodicals. Finally, to protect the petitioners against reprisals by the government, the petition was burned.

Word of the abysmal role of the IDB soon got out. Two hundred and ten Canadian missionaries in Haiti sent a telegram to then Prime Minister Pierre Trudeau, protesting Canada's participation in financing the dam,[21] and human rights groups in France, Canada, and the U.S. put pressure on their own governments to open up the review process and to consider alternatives to the dams. Adding to this pressure was the growing attention the project was getting in the international press. The prestigious Paris-based journal, *Le Monde diplomatique*, condemned the dams as a "deliberate sacrifice of agriculture to the needs of .... the foreign factories in the capital."[22]

Then quietly one day, sometime in late 1983, the Government of Haiti and the IDB "decided to postpone implementing the study's recommendations for [the first dam] until 1990, with the implementation of the recommendations for [the second dam] being postponed indefinitely."[23]

The opposition to the dams had won a temporary victory, temporary because the dam plans are not dead, only dormant. When they are revived the Haitian peasants will be forced to resume their highly vocal and dangerous opposition efforts. The lessons the peasants have learned is that they cannot trust their own government or international aid agencies, because they do not respond to reasoned arguments in a public forum but only to opposition expressed in a highly vocal way.

This is the same lesson that the Kalinga tribal people in the Philippines have learned, after they saw how little regard their government and the World Bank had for their homes and sacred lands. But in the case of the 85,000 Kalinga and Bontoc, their opposition to the Chico Dams has taken on a much broader, anti-government perspective. Despite the Kalinga's reluctance to associate with outsiders, reports from anthropologists and church activists in the Philippines now indicate that these fiercely independent people have gradually responded to promises of help from the New People's Army, the armed guerrilla wing of the Communist Party of the Philippines, "because it seemed to offer them hope in the face of the overwhelming forces arrayed against them."[24]

Like the Haitian dams, the Chico dams have been postponed because of the international outcry but the people of the Chico River Valley feel no more security than the

Haitians do. The power lines and the irrigation canals that would feed off the Chico dams have "already begun to march across the neighboring, lowland provinces," according to anthropologist Charles Drucker, "carrying with them the certainty of another bloody confrontation in the not-too-distant future."[25]

The conflicts in the Philippines and in Haiti have been underway for more than five years, but the secretive process which has, by its very nature, led to these conflicts shows no signs of reform. The secrecy of aid agencies[26] is made all the more disturbing by the reluctance of elected officials in some countries to accept responsibility when details of a project gone askew get out.

When questioned by the public about Canadian support for the Haitian dams through its vote in the IDB, the Minister for External Affairs, Allan MacEachen, pointed out that the IDB, not Canada, was funding the dams.[27] As Canada is a minority voting member who contributes a minority of the cost, he absolved the Canadian government of responsibility in the IDB's projects.

American foreign aid officials have not been able to disclaim responsibility for multilateral bank projects: they have had to account for U.S. participation in these banks before two congressional committees which began hearings in 1983 on the environmental impact of their projects.[28] American officials have also been pressured by a coalition of environmental and indigenous rights groups, representing over five million Americans, to either insure that the environmental and social review process of the multilateral development banks is improved or to withdraw U.S. contributions to the banks.

Calls for aid agencies to be more responsible have also come from other quarters: the Brandt Commission said that "we stress the need to make aid-giving organizations more accountable, and comprehensible, to politicians and publics in all countries;"[29] the *Guardian* called the World Bank, in particular, "a mystery, accountable to no one."[30]

Recognizing the absence of accountability, the World Bank's Goodland encouraged environmentalists and human rights advocates "to alert the financiers and the development agencies and the national governments to some of the unforeseen side effects, and work with them to try and improve their planning."[31] But the best information is invariably at the local level, with the people to be affected by a project.

Until aid givers and aid receivers recognize that public review of development projects is not an obstacle to development but an essential stage in a process that helps root out potential mistakes and enfranchises people with a say in their own destiny, foreign aid will continue to be an instrument of harm. Nothing of substance will have been learned.

# PART III

# Technological Fixes: Myths About What The Third World Needs

# 11

## *We need to switch to nuclear power to save the world's scarce resources for the Third World*

"If the rich industrial nations wish to help the developing world, they should build uranium power plants, so as to make fossil fuels more available and less costly for the small users."
— Chauncey Starr, at the 7th Annual Symposium of the Uranium Institute in London, September 1982.

"How, then, can the oil savings so central to security and world peace be reliably achieved without nuclear power? Broadly speaking, the important oil saving measures are distressingly simple: stop driving Petropigs and stop living in sieves."
— Amory and Hunter Lovins, in *Energy/War: Breaking the Nuclear Link.*

IF THE AFFLUENT NATIONS don't switch to nuclear power, proponents of nuclear power have claimed, and we continue to blindly burn dwindling fossil fuels as if they aren't dwindling, it won't be we in the rich and powerful nations who will suffer but the poor in the Third World: we'll always have enough money to buy the oil we need to keep our economies growing, but the Third World won't. To prevent their economies from being forever doomed, we should, on moral grounds if nothing else, embrace nuclear power to conserve fossil fuels for the needy countries.

This piece of conventional wisdom, which differs little from the conventional wisdom that nuclear power is needed to help get us off oil for our own good, is disproved daily: nuclear power, which produces electricity, does not save oil.

North America has a huge surplus of electricity — about 40 percent continent-wide.[1] If surplus electricity could replace significant quantities of the oil we burn, it would have done so. Building more nuclear reactors would only create a larger surplus of electricity and do nothing to convince people to switch away from the oil and gas that they currently prefer over electricity to heat homes, fuel industries, and run cars.

If nuclear power is to make major inroads in replacing the oil we consume, it will have to become useful in transportation — the single biggest consumer of oil. But barring major technological advances, massive subsidization, and possibly even a restructuring of our economy, nuclear power is wholly impractical as a transportation fuel. Electric automobiles are no more feasible today than they were half a century ago because batteries have yet to be developed which are powerful enough, light enough, and cheap enough to move today's cars and trucks far enough or fast enough. Even with a breathtaking technological breakthrough, consumers would be asked to change their habits considerably. Among the more plausible schemes proposed in the event of such a breakthrough are overnight recharging of batteries in garages, "battery bars" where consumers swap discharged batteries for recharged ones, and new designs for cities to reduce traveling distances to levels compatible with a battery's range.

Without electric batteries, nuclear electricity could become a transportation fuel if the car was rejected for mass transit through a switch to electric buses, streetcars, and subways. But this would probably require forced changes in consumer habits, in the way cities work, and in the functioning of major sectors of the economy like the automotive industry.

Next to transportation, the best prospect for nuclear electricity is in replacing oil heating. But this would also require massive subsidies because nuclear reactors — which are designed to run flat out, 24 hours a day, all year long, to keep costs down — do not match the home heating needs of consumers, which vary with the hour and the season. Nuclear reactors could not be sensibly built for a peak requirement like heating because they would sit idle most of the time, pricing themselves out of the market.

When nuclear electricity tries to replace non-electrical fuels, it fails abysmally. But it also fails to replace other electrical fuels, such as oil- or coal-generated electricity.

According to the electricity industry in the U.S., power from nuclear reactors coming on line from 1983 to the early 1990s will cost up to 50 percent more than power from comparable coal plants. The Electric Power Research Institute, which represents privately owned utilities, has found that "commercial nuclear plants have turned out to be much more expensive than coal plants," and Charles Komanoff, a New York-based energy consultant, has concluded that electricity from new reactors will cost an average of 80 percent more than electricity from coal, a difference totalling $2 billion over the life of a typical new plant. New nuclear plants should not be built, he said, "unless there are stunning changes in a stunning number of circumstances."[2]

If the purpose of all the extra costs and social upheavals involved in switching to nuclear power is to make sure the Third World can afford to buy oil, it would be far cheaper for us, and far less coercive on us, to simply provide the Third World with the necessary cash.

Nuclear power has another drawback which limits its usefulness in getting off oil: to build a nuclear plant requires ten to 14 years, making it useless in response to a crisis. Partly for this reason, shortly after the OPEC oil crisis hit in 1973, electric utilities across the continent began to abandon nuclear power. Since 1976, every new nuclear power station that has been ordered in North America, and thousands which had earlier been on the drawing boards, have been shelved.[3] Despite the wild optimism that nuclear power would become the fuel of the future, and the billions in subsidies that have already been poured into it, nuclear power has proven to be so impractical and expensive that it now accounts for only three percent of North America's energy consumption, compared to about 75 percent for oil and gas. This failure on the part of nuclear power did not, however, prevent the West from cutting back dramatically on its use of the world's oil supplies.

In just one decade after the OPEC oil crisis, the world has gone from energy shortages to energy surpluses, thanks mostly to conservation. OPEC now produces only 17 million barrels a day — as little as it produced during the 1960s and down from a high of 31 million barrels a day in 1979. Canada has become self-sufficient in oil and the United States imports less than it did in 1973. Conservation has also been a driving force in Europe, where it has provided 95 percent of all the new energy "discovered" in the five-year period since OPEC.[4] The remaining five percent, which received most of the capital expenditures and virtually all of the government subsidies, came from new oil and gas finds, such as those in the North Sea, and from the new nuclear power plants brought on stream. Although the North Sea has no trifling amount of oil, and nuclear plants are large suppliers of electricity, they are dwarfed to insignificance when seen against the contribution of conservation. It would have required 20 North Sea finds, and 20 times as many nuclear plants, to have fuelled the same growth in the EEC's economy without conservation.

Thanks to conservation, and no thanks to nuclear power, the West's use of oil has continued to fall each year, while its economic growth continues to climb. These oil savings benefit people everywhere but especially those in Third World countries whose balance of payments have deteriorated greatly as a result of the oil crisis. In 1972, only 1.5 percent of Kenya's export earnings were needed to import oil. By 1980, that figure had climbed to 36 percent.[5] For the poor countries as a whole, the oil bill has shot up from $7 billion in 1973 to about $67 billion in 1980,[6] hurting over 100 Third World countries which produce no oil at all and another 13 which import at least 45 percent of their oil.

But action by the West can never be enough. The Third World needs to secure energy independence for itself, and that can only come from developing its own energy supplies. What those supplies should be is a matter of hot debate that has people championing every alternative under the sun, including nuclear power.

# 12

## *The Third World needs nuclear power because it can't afford oil*

"To say that Third World countries cannot use nuclear energy is also a mistake. Giant cities, such as Calcutta, Rio de Janeiro, Mexico City, Jakarta and many others could use nuclear energy to great advantage."
— Edward Teller, father of the U.S. hydrogen bomb, quoted in the *Globe and Mail*, July 14, 1980.

"Taking nuclear power to the Third World is like taking a 12-mm gun to a fly."
— Ishrat Usmani, a former Pakistani official who helped set up his country's nuclear power program, but resigned when military designs overtook civilian concerns. Quoted in *WISE*, June 1982.

IF THE THIRD WORLD can't afford oil, it can't afford nuclear power, because nuclear power is only cheap under one condition: when the primary purpose of the nuclear reactor is to produce plutonium for nuclear bombs and whatever electricity is generated comes as a bonus. When this military purpose is not present, and power for commercial uses is the objective, nuclear reactors can't compete with oil, gas, or other options a country might have.

Argentina is one country that has admitted as much. According to Miguel S. Ussher in 1982, an assistant to the Argentine President, building nuclear reactors could not be justified without the military component to Argentina's nuclear power program:

> There are many other ways we could put the money in a better way. For example, let's suppose gas turbines. Since we have 70 years' reserve of gas, we could go into gas turbines and we could cover the country with gas turbines and that would solve all the problems. We know that perfectly, and [gas] would cost less....[nuclear] electricity is the most expensive one. But from other points of view....technically speaking it was very convenient for us. Not economically.[1]

Other countries that have embarked on commercial nuclear power programs are also on record as desiring nuclear weapons capability. Pakistan's former President, Ali Bhutto, said his countrymen would "eat leaves or grass" to obtain nuclear weapons, and according to CIA intelligence, the Candu reactor Canada sold the Pakistanis made Bhutto's dream achievable.[2] The Chinese government vowed in 1963 that it would get the bomb "even if it ends up with no money to produce trousers."[3] Other countries that are obtaining the West's nuclear power technology have not admitted military intentions, but most are threatened nations in militarily unstable regions. This includes such countries as Romania,

Taiwan, and South Korea, which have obtained Canadian nuclear technology; Iraq, which has French nuclear technology; the Philippines which has American nuclear technology; and Cuba which is obtaining Soviet nuclear technology. India, the first country to receive Candu technology, used it to explode a nuclear bomb in 1974.[4]

If not for its military usefulness, nuclear reactors would be the least suited way for Third World countries to produce electricity. These countries are chronically short of capital, and what a nuclear power system needs most is capital: up to $3 billion per reactor can be required, an amount greater than the gross national product of countries like Jamaica or Senegal.

Even bigger and relatively richer Third World nations like Mexico and Brazil have been forced to cut back or abandon their nuclear programs because they were an economic burden. Under pressure from the International Monetary Fund, Brazil in 1981 cut back its ambitious $24 billion nuclear expansion program from nine reactors to four[5] while Mexico in 1982 called off its entire $30 billion nuclear energy program because, as one senior government official put it, it would be "suicide" for the country to go ahead with its nuclear program when it has "lots of cheap oil." Although the West's nuclear exporters were outdoing themselves, offering Third World countries greater and greater subsidies to purchase their reactors, one industry spokesman from the U.S. said quite simply that "they couldn't pay for them."[6]

Relatively well-off Taiwan and South Korea, after a decade of nuclear expansion programs, have paid a price for their ambitions. According to Yoon Hyungkim, head of a group set up by the governments of Japan, Taiwan, and South Korea to assess the future of electricity in Asia, these three countries of the Far East, like the Western nations, greatly overbuilt their systems. After finding themselves carrying the heavy burden of excess capacities varying between 40 percent and 60 percent, "they are certainly learning from past mistakes," Hyungkim says.[7] "One lesson is that they are planning fewer and smaller plants, focussing on conservation and flexibility."

In addition to the economic inappropriateness of nuclear power, it is technically inappropriate for all but a handful of developing countries. Nuclear reactors, which are designed to be very large to keep costs down, require a large electric power grid to provide reliable service. Very few Third World countries have grids large enough. Even India's relatively small 200-megawatt RAPP-1 reactor caused the entire grid it feeds to collapse several times, and needed to be run at half power to avoid other collapses.[8] In contrast, the reactors now being built in Canada produce 850 megawatts, those in the U.S. produce over 1,000 megawatts.

As a result of these economic and technical handicaps, nuclear power has not penetrated commercial markets in the Third World and is unlikely to in future, according to a study by the Worldwatch Institute. The economics of nuclear power have worsened over time, largely due to the need for additional safety features. Over the past decade the amount of concrete, piping, and cable used in an average nuclear plant has more than doubled, and labor requirements have more than tripled. These and a host of other factors have raised the costs of new U.S. reactors to six times the cost of plants finished before the 1973 oil embargo, even taking inflation into account. Electricity from new nuclear plants, which now costs ten to twelve cents per kilowatt hour — more than that from oil-generating plants — will reach 14 to 16 cents in 1990. The cost of a kilowatt-hour generated by burning coal will be roughly half that amount in both years.[9]

Exports of 'mini-reactors' of 50 to 200 megawatts to the Third World, on which the West's nuclear industry is pinning its hopes for a rebirth, are also uncompetitive. Although they are meant to expand the potential market by up to 100 reactors in more than 56 additional Third World nations, their price-tags, starting at a half-billion dollars, make the power from these reactors more costly than power from the conventional large reactors, and still more expensive than a variety of cheaper and environmentally more benign alternatives for generating or saving electric power.[10]

Among those alternatives are coal stations with acid-gas emission controls, small-scale hydroelectric stations, industrial and commercial cogeneration, and conservation by reducing transmission losses. The World Bank estimates that Third World countries lose almost twice as much as they should in their transmission and distribution systems and that it is "nearly three times cheaper to save one kilowatt of electricity by improving the distribution system than to produce an additional kilowatt from new generating equipment."[11]

Aside from plutonium for military uses, nuclear reactors can only effectively produce electricity. They cannot replace the oil that is used to move cars and trucks, which account for 50 percent to 60 percent of the Third World's total oil consumption.[12] Without energy conservation in the transportation sector, Third World countries are unlikely to see any significant dent in their oil-induced foreign debts.

But nuclear energy represents more than just another power form. Like the electricity it produces, it is equated with industrialization, and seen as a catalyst to progress. The magic of electricity writ large is embodied by nuclear reactors producing power for dense urban populations. The same magic writ small is distributing power from large, central generating stations to remote hamlets in the low density, rural areas.

# 13

## *Rural electrification will transform the depressed and stagnant rural areas of the Third World into healthy economic centres; it will increase agricultural output, promote rural industries, create rural employment, lower birth rates, and improve the quality of rural life*

"I don't think there is any program which will help [the Third World] more than this."
— President John F. Kennedy, witnessing the signing of a foreign aid contract for rural electrification, November 1, 1962.

"Rural electrification from centralized sources in the Third World is rarely a success story."
— Amulya Reddy, Indian Institute of Science, Bangalore, in 1981.

THE WORLD'S FIRST great introduction to rural electrification as a panacea for "underdevelopment" was made with the inauguration of the Tennessee Valley Authority, America's largest utility. The TVA was to provide, among other services, the electricity thought necessary for regional economic development. By most accounts (most of them originating with David Lilienthal, the power expert on the TVA Board), the TVA "saved the Valley from economic despair and made it a cornucopia."[1] But more disinterested observers are coming to different conclusions.

A recent book, *The Myth of the TVA*, by William Chandler of the Washington-based Environmental Policy Institute, shows that the TVA provided no greater economic growth for the region than occurred in similar areas which did not receive any of the TVA's massive funding.[2] Even more surprising to those who have grown up with the myth of the TVA, rural electrification proceeded more slowly in the TVA area than in nearby states.

According to this book, which reviewed the TVA's 50-year history, the reason is straightforward. People use electricity only as they can afford to and, compared to other rural parts of the nation which were electrifying more rapidly, the TVA region was relatively poor. Development and affluence bring about the desire for electrical services, Chandler explains, not vice versa.[3]

Rural electrification can provide many benefits. But because its proponents have zealously adopted it as their mission and credited it with almost magical powers, it has been pushed to the exclusion of other energy forms.

Worldwide, the belief is prevalent that rural electrification acts as a catalyst to raise food production, trigger agricultural and small-scale industrial development, increase employment, reduce migration to urban centers, and even curb population growth. As if it were borrowing a script from the promotional pieces of the TVA, the Philippines National Electrification Administration described in its 1979 Annual Report how rural electrification

> has transformed sleepy and apathetic rural villages into industrial and commercial beehives .... rural electrification indeed is the most dramatic symbol of the quantum jump of the Philippines into modernization. With rural electrification many farmers are now set on running their irrigation pumps. With government encouragement, small and medium-scale industries are sprouting all over the archipelago.[4]

A few dissenting words are occasionally heard, however. A 1983 study of rural electrification programs by the International Labor Organization[5] could find no evidence to support the claims made for rural electrification. What the ILO did find was that cumulative investments in Third World electrification, estimated at between $10 and $20 billion,[6] has resulted in little electrification actually occurring. This confirmed the World Bank's discovery, ten years earlier, that only twelve percent of the Third World's population had access to electricity.[7] But having access does not mean that they use it. Only one half of that twelve percent, according to the Worldwatch Institute, could afford to purchase the power available,[8] confirming the ILO's conclusion that the rural poor have not benefitted substantially from the advent of electric power to their villages. As an editorial in India's *Economic and Political Weekly* explains, the reason why electricity is used in only ten to twelve percent of India's 2,300,000 households that are officially classified as electrified is....

> altogether simple: the electrification of rural households requires the installation of main metres

> and other equipment along with internal wiring which calls for an investment of between 500 and 800 rupees per household [nearly half the annual per capita income] at the very least. Obviously, the overwhelming majority of the rural population, consisting of agricultural laborers, small peasants and tenants, rural artisans, etc. is in no position to make this investment.[9]

Eighty percent of the Third World's electricity is supplied from a central grid,[10] which links the electricity generating stations to large urban populations. To bring electricity to areas distant from the grid — the remote communities with low population densities and few uses for electricity — is prohibitively expensive. Even if people were to have their homes wired for free, most could afford to buy precious little electricity.

Even subsidized, as it usually is, electricity is a "luxury good," according to the ILO. The only ones who tend to benefit from the subsidies in countries as different as Papua New Guinea, Bolivia, and India are the larger farms and wealthier families — the only ones who can afford the electricity. As the Papua New Guinea government explained in its 1978 energy policy paper:

> The research we have conducted into the distribution of existing energy forms in Papua New Guinea villages informs us that a relative few, the wealthier villagers, benefit most, and these families will certainly be the first, and perhaps the only beneficiaries of rural electrification. Because rural electrification would have to be heavily subsidized in Papua New Guinea, it could well turn into a

> subsidy of only the well off. Rural electrification is likely to be a much more effective instrument creating rural elites than could be the case with investment in schools, roads and other community facilities.[11]

In Nicaragua, the failure of rural electrification is similar. "Only on the largest, most heavily capitalized farms and ranches in the three cooperative areas was electricity used for production or processing purposes,"[12] reports Development Alternatives Inc., which also found no evidence that electricity was a factor in starting these activities, or that it was cheaper.

Advocates of rural electrification are also starting to discover that their dreams are not being realized. A study of 23 rural communities of Colombia, Peru, and Chile for AID, America's foreign aid agency and one of the world's leading proponents of rural electrification, found that:

> .... in spite of the universal belief that electrification means progress, none of the electrified sites visited could report any positive economic impact attributable to the installation of electric power .... Although questioned hopefully on other measures of "progress" .... increased literacy, some minimal industrialization, etc., the answers were essentially negative. The provision of electrification had not proven sufficient to trigger economic development.[13]

Confirming this finding is another AID study of rural electrification in Bolivia which found that electricity was neither a catalyst nor a precondition for economic develop-

ment of rural areas.[14] The Inter-American Development Bank has come to the same conclusions. In a major evaluation of its $414 million loans to 25 rural electrification projects in nine Latin American countries, the Inter-American Development Bank found no "general agreement or substantial evidence" that gains in agricultural productivity, their goal, were the results of the projects.[15]

The often-made claim that rural electrification leads to an increase in employment is also difficult to support. After reviewing many cases, the International Labor Organization study concluded that "there is not much evidence to suggest that electricity which is used for productive purposes has so far had any major beneficial impact on the employment/income situation of the rural poor. On the contrary, there is some evidence of net job-losses and of a worsening income distribution as a result of rural electrification."

In India, for example, most farmers now using electricity were able to release members of their family or hired labor from irrigation tasks. In the rural areas of Java and the Philippines, the coconut oil manufacturing industries are using electricity to displace thousands of workers. Apart from a few cases, such as in China where rural manufacturing and service industries absorbed surplus labor, the evidence indicates that the workers who were displaced in most Third World countries generally found no alternative employment.

As for the popular theory that rural electrification acts as a brake on migration to urban areas, the ILO study voted no confidence here as well. AID concurred: it found that in Costa Rica electrification had a neutral effect on migration patterns.[16]

Exuberance for the attributes of rural electrification extends beyond the economic factors to social ones, such as population control. Said an Indian Minister, "in the dark villages, the only recreation at night is procreation,"[17] and in Pakistan, a Planning Director for the Water and Power Development Authority put it like this: ".... perhaps a most important effect of rural electrification which has largely gone unnoticed has been in the area of population control. It is generally true in Pakistan that wherever electricity has been supplied, the population growth rate has fallen noticeably."[18] Here again, credit is given where credit is not due. Electricity is used by people who can afford it — by those who are better off — and in Pakistan those who are better off are also tending to have fewer children.[19]

In addition to the $10 or $20 billion dollars already spent on Third World rural electrification, as much as $65 billion has been slated to be spent in the 1980s,[20] yet, says the ILO, there is not so much as "a few success stories" to justify these expenditures ".... such stories do not yet exist." Crediting electrification with the powers to develop a rural community "is difficult, if not impossible."[21]

Rural electrification from large central stations is still pushed as an answer to the Third World's problems, but the ardor behind the push is waning. Another form of rural electrification, based on a decentralized energy technology, has become the darling instead, and it is quickly attracting the attention of business interests as well as political leaders. The technology is solar power, an obvious choice, its proponents reason, because if there's one thing the Third World has plenty of it's sun.

# 14

## *We should export our solar technology to the Third World*

"Despite its present size, and a technology that is virtually untested in many applications, the market [for solar power] is predicted to be explosive."
— From *Crain's Cleveland Business*, reproduced in the *Report on Business*, May 4, 1984.

"Anyone who has lived or traveled outside the cities in the Third World has seen the ruins of biodigesters or the skeletons of windmills long since abandoned."
— James Howe of the Overseas Development Council, in the *EPRI Journal*, July/August 1980.

WE CAN'T SELL ANY technology, no matter how sensible it may seem to us, to unwilling customers or to customers who can't afford to buy it. The huge Third World market imagined by the West's solar salesmen is neither willing nor able to purchase our solar technology.

Yet this hasn't stopped the business press from trumpeting the potential market for solar power in the Third World. "[Solar] pumpers key to billion-dollar market" in the *Renewable Energy News*, an international trade newspaper, reports that solar pumps are becoming so cheap and easy to operate that they could replace the millions of hand pumps being promoted to Third World farmers by the world's aid agencies.[1] "Foreign markets are main outlet for Canadian solar expertise," a full-color, front-page article in the *Globe and Mail Report on Business*,[2] sings the praises of a $10 million solar export industry that is heating homes in Egypt, removing sea salt from the Indian Ocean for Kenyans, and satisfying a host of residential needs in the Caribbean. In another *Report on Business* article,[3] the *Globe* claims that

> [B]igger opportunities [for our solar industry] lie in the developing world, which is now paying a total of $50 billion a year for energy and desperately wants to find alternatives that will save money and make it less dependent on outside supplies .... There is a lot of money to be made once the developing world becomes fully aware of the solar alternative.

Politicians primed by the solar industry have joined in the fervor of spreading the solar gospel to the Third World. At the United Nations 1981 conference, *New and Renewable Sources of Energy*, held in Nairobi, Kenya, official delegates from countries around the world agreed on the need to promote the development of renewable energy technologies.

Canadian Prime Minister Trudeau, in a keynote address, committed $40 million to the development of these technologies to relieve the plight of the "two-and-one-half billion of the world's poorest people, the great majority of whom live in rural areas [and] depend for almost all of their energy needs upon wood, agricultural residues, and dung — the so-called non-commercial fuels."[4]

Energy Minister Marc Lalonde also stressed Canada's commitment to the solar cause, and even at the provincial level solar enthusiasts could be found. Ontario Energy Minister Robert Welch left the Nairobi conference exuberant about his province's potential for selling alternative energy technologies abroad. "We've got a great future offshore," he said. "The emphasis on new and renewable energy resources means a new source of jobs for us."[5] To underline his commitment, Welch announced $2.5 million in solar grants designed to nurture the fledgling solar manufacturers who are expected to be among the future export leaders.

As a result of this unanimity among the governments of industrialized countries, the view that Third World countries are perfectly suited for renewable energy technologies has been enshrined in virtually all of their policy statements. This view is especially strong with regard to the rural areas of the Third World where isolated populations often depend on expensive energy sources such as oil- or diesel-generated electricity, or where rural populations simply do without these energy sources.

The presumption that the Third World was desperately in need of Western solar technology created a plethora of poorly thought-out foreign aid projects that, according to an unpublished internal World Bank working paper, led to numerous failures. The testing of technologies was limited to favorable circumstances, the needs of the ultimate consumers were largely ignored, and little attention was paid to whether the products could be manufactured locally, marketed locally, or even repaired locally. "The demonstration projects have tended to become ends in themselves,"[6] the document concluded.

Another study showed that of some 175 renewable energy projects planned or carried out by a variety of aid agencies in Africa, 77 percent of the total expenditures went to projects producing and installing solar equipment while only 23 percent went to projects determining what solar applications would be useful to Third World consumers.[7]

According to a report prepared for the United Nations Commission for Trade and Development, there is an "unmistakable .... bias towards hardware projects," and a "misplaced or at least premature" rush to get systems out into the field for testing and demonstration.[8]

In Mali, where American, Canadian, and European aid agencies funded a project to test solar-powered water pumps, more pumps were installed than were needed for research and development purposes, and no record was kept of their performance.[9] In Mexico, where the French set up a series of solar irrigation pumps, the yield was a series of failures. "The project," according to a former director of the U.N. Environment Program's Latin American Office, "has proved to be very profitable for the French and costly to the Mexicans. It does not generate employment, there is an increasing dependency on foreign technologies, it is capital-intensive. And contrary to the long life expected, in less than five years of operation only one of the 13 plants is still in operation."[10]

With all these failures, there is little wonder that the West's development strategy for the solar industry has not been universally appreciated by Third World recipients. Anil Agarwal, Director of India's Centre for Science and Environment, speaks for many when he asserts that "the list of immature technologies that developing countries have been pushed and cajoled into buying is long."[11]

The fears of people in the Third World that they are being used as guinea pigs are reinforced by programs like the Canadian International Development Agency's $15 million plan to place photovoltaic water pumping systems in remote regions of six African nations. The Canadian consultants who will get the contracts will be on a learning assignment. According to *Renewable Energy News*, before Canadian companies can "cash in on the CIDA money and the growing Third World market," they will have to do some basic research. The National Research Council is putting up the money to pay for this necessary step because, as an NRC official described it, "at this stage Canadians need the experience of putting together systems. We're newcomers at this thing, so the research money is needed to position companies to take advantage of the CIDA contracts when they come up."[12]

The solar industry hasn't seen the failed demonstration projects, or the market resistance to its motherhood products. Like everyone else, it became caught up in the euphoria about the multi-billion dollar export market that was supposed to be just around the corner, and projected future sales on the basis of this apparently lucrative market. "The trouble with the industry is that no one asks what would happen if three billion people [in the Third World] who don't have electricity today can't afford photovoltaics," said Exxon Vice-President John Wurmser, one of the first industry members to grasp the problem, in announcing the failure of Exxon's solar photovoltaic subsidiary, Solar Power Corporation.[13] After $30 million invested, Exxon decided the photovoltaic market would not penetrate the Third World's rural areas fast enough or profitably enough for the oil giant. With industry overcapacity between 300 percent and 500 percent, Exxon has left the field to Amoco, Sohio, and the other companies that are still euphoric about their sales prospects selling to the largely cashless poor in the Third World.

Lack of cash, however, may be only part of the problem. Even if all the solar technology the Third World needs could be financed by aid agencies, Third World critics such as Arnoldo Ventura, Executive Director of Jamaica's Science Research Council, maintain that "most technologies developed in industrialized countries are inappropriate and irrelevant to developing countries." Fearing the indiscriminate adoption of the West's energy technologies, he warns that "even if technologies were tried and tested, their mere import at give-away prices would do little more than create an appetite and increase dependence. The solution is to develop new and renewable energy technologies in developing countries."[14]

This solution is hard for anyone to quarrel with. But some take Ventura's reasoning a large step further. They note the many problems the West experienced during the Industrial Revolution after it switched from wood to coal, and then later after it switched to oil and gas for the energy it needed to drive its economy. Ultimately, everyone will be switching to solar power, they argue, so the Third World should go directly there, and skip all the expensive, polluting, and obsolete steps in between.

# 15

## *The Third World should skip the oil era and get directly onto renewable energy*

"The Third World, however, has an advantage in that it can take a shortcut past the fossil fuel cul-de-sac."
– Denis Hayes, *Energy for Development: Third World Options*, Worldwatch, 1977.

"The conference is not an attempt to turn the developing countries to alternate sources of energy so that the remaining oil reserves would be available to the industrialized world. Poor nations .... will continue to require oil and coal."
– Uruguay's Enrique V. Iglesias, head of a U.N. Conference on New and Renewable Sources of Energy, reassures Third World delegates of the conference's motives, August, 1981.

THE THIRD WORLD now relies on renewable forms of energy: in fact, it already utilizes small-scale, decentralized forms of energy for the majority of its needs. The poor in these countries can afford little else.

In Ethiopia, 96 percent of the total energy consumed is supplied by wood and other agricultural wastes.[1] In Kenya, over 90 percent of the population depends on woodfuel and charcoal to meet its domestic energy needs.[2] Fuelwood alone contributes 96 percent of the energy used in Tanzania, 91 percent in Nigeria, and 90 percent in Uganda.[3] For Africa as a whole, 89 percent of the total energy used comes from renewable sources. In Asia it is 50 percent; Latin America, 51 percent; and for the Third World as a whole, the figure is 52 percent.[4]

Most of the modern fuels like coal, oil, or electricity that are used in the Third World are consumed in cities, primarily by vehicles, commercial enterprises, and industry. For the bulk of the Third World's population, these commercial fuels are luxuries that can be used only sparingly, if at all.

In a typical Indian village of 500 or fewer residents (60 percent of India's 567,000 villages fall in this category), biomass such as firewood, corn stalks, or cow dung accounts for more than two thirds of the village's energy consumption. Animal power, generally in the form of bullocks pulling a plow or cart, provides another 15 percent, and human labor for plowing and harvesting accounts for ten percent. All commercial fuels combined amount to only seven percent of the village's consumption: oil at four percent, electricity at two percent, and coal at one percent.[5]

In agriculture, the little commercial energy that is used runs irrigation pumps. But the importance of commercial energy pales next to that of human and animal power,[6] which together account for 90 percent of the total energy used in agriculture.

If the goal of Third World countries was to become all-renewable-energy societies, they would not have far to go compared to the rest of the world. But progress and development cannot be measured by this yardstick alone. A country like India, which uses one ninth the energy per person that is consumed in the developed world, will need additional energy services to reduce the backbreaking human energy required for agriculture, to increase irrigation for crops, and to provide lighting for the home.

These additional energy services can be provided both by increasing the efficiency with which present energy supplies are used and by simply increasing the energy supplies available, whether renewable or non-renewable. Based on the work of Amulya Reddy at the Indian Institute of Science, we estimate that a ten-percent increase in the efficiency with which human and animal power is used in agriculture — through the use of better levers and pulleys, for example — would yield as much extra energy as a doubling of all the commercial energy an Indian village uses in agriculture.[7]

Conservation of commercial fuels in the industrial and urban sectors would yield similarly large gains. But when industry and individuals consume as little energy as they do in India, there is a limit to how many of the additional energy services they need can be fueled by the energy saved through conservation.

Beyond those efficiency improvements still to be tapped, more energy resources will need to be used if standards of living are to be raised. What kinds of energy are used when by people in the Third World should depend not on ideology but on which energy sources are available and economical for the task. Wherever diesel generators produce electricity more cheaply and reliably than solar cells, whenever gasoline is preferable to gasohol for cars, it makes little sense to opt for renewable energy: a wholesale, immediate conversion to renewable energy — for them as for us — should not be a goal in itself but a means to a more efficient and environmentally sustainable energy future.

# 16

## *Third World people don't know what is in their own self-interest. Look at the way they squander woodfuel, for example*

"Every log she gathers contributes to the degradation of the environment, contributing to the spread of deserts and arid areas .... The answer .... is to produce more efficient fuelwood stoves."
— "Better stoves help solve fuelwood crisis," *Christian Science Monitor*, March 14, 1984.

"The rural poor are unlikely to use it even if it is given free to them."
— Mohan Parikh, the first promoter of the box-type solar cooker as an alternative to inefficient wood stoves, no longer is confident of its usefulness.

IMAGINE THE FOLLY of some experts from Africa flying to New York or Toronto on a three-week fact-finding mission to tell North Americans how to maximize their use of energy. In a few weeks the African experts would draw together all the data, analyze it, and then write a report that would explain the ways North Americans are squandering their precious resources and, as a result, acting against their own self-interest.

Though the Africans' advice may be well intentioned, they can hardly be expected to understand the many factors behind the energy systems that have evolved here. Why some of us use oil to heat our homes and others use electricity. Why some communities burn wood and others ban it. Why some utilities are privately owned, and others are publicly owned. Why nuclear plants can be found in some high population areas, but not in others. No one would be surprised if their advice were not taken.

In practice, Third World experts rarely fly to Western countries offering advice. Western experts, on the other hand, regularly fly to Third World countries, armed with everything but an understanding of the rationale behind the systems they are trying to replace, modernize, or otherwise improve.

In the past decade, the attention of the West's energy experts has increasingly focussed on the single biggest consumer of wood energy in the Third World: the woodstove. Literally hundreds of more efficient cooking stove designs[1] have been developed in the West by many highly trained technical experts.

But the designs fail. The solar-powered cooker is one example of a product that is efficient technically — it runs on nothing more than the rays of the sun — and useless practically.[2] In the Third World, as in the West, women do most of the cooking, and they prefer to cook at the end of the day, not at noon, which is the optimal time to use solar cookers. They also like to cook when it is cool, not under the tropical noonday sun. Beyond the inconvenience, midday cooking would require that women stop cultivating their farms, which most could not afford to do.

Less exotic stoves, quite similar to the traditional stove only up to four times more efficient, also fail. Many of the stoves seem sensible by any standard: they often are made out of local materials, are easy to repair, and cost no more than traditional stoves. Yet when such an expertly designed stove is given to a Third World family to try out over an extended period of time, the traditional stove proves more useful and the new one almost always ends up as a mere curiosity. As it turns out, there is more to the Third World stove than meets the eye.

The traditional charcoal stove is a utensil that often does more than provide heat for cooking. In the Kenyan capital of Nairobi, the stove (typically the same size, but of a different shape, than a hibachi) is used outside before dusk to cook the evening meal. After dusk, when the temperature drops, the stove — its coals no longer smoking but burning white with heat — is brought inside to warm the home and boil the water for tea. Elsewhere in the Third World, the stove's smoke is used to repel bugs or to preserve thatched roofs, and the glow of the fire plays the same social role that our own fireplaces do. In other words, depending on the climate, type of home, and cultural habits of different communities, the cooking stove doubles as a space heater, fireplace, insect repellent, and preservative.[3]

For a new technology to succeed in replacing this multipurpose household utensil, it must provide all these services, or at least large enough savings that any foregone service can be affordably provided in other ways. Little wonder, then, that Western efforts at producing stoves that increase the efficiency of only one of their functions — their cooking efficiency — at the expense of their other functions, have met with dismal results. When people in colder parts of the Third World do use high-efficiency cooking stoves, which don't give off much waste heat, they often compensate with an open fire that consumes the BTUs that the more efficient cooking stove saves.

The experts' error lay with their assumption that they understood what the Third World needed — an assumption based on nothing more than a conviction that Western know-how, which could put a man on the moon, would be capable of solving something as simple as the Third World's cooking fuel shortage. In the experts' enthusiasm to produce the product they assumed the Third World had been waiting for, they neglected to conduct the basic market research that would be commonplace in the West — for example, asking the women who would be using the stoves whether they suited their needs.

Market research is a sophisticated business of trying to determine the factors behind other peoples' thinking in order to determine what is or is not saleable about a potential new product. It is difficult for North Americans even when dealing with their own culture. When dealing with an altogether foreign culture, it approaches the impossible. A Westerner, especially a technical expert from a foreign aid agency without marketing savvy and aloof from the everyday concerns of Third World consumers, is not likely to ascertain how they think, any more than an African expert is likely to understand what we want in our kitchen appliances.

Western experts are further handicapped by the alien workings of woodstove markets in the Third World. In the urban centers, the market is large for inexpensive stoves but almost non-existent for ones that could be mass produced by a large manufacturing concern. A cast-iron, energy efficient stove that could be produced in Nairobi would cost about $30 compared to the $3 cost of a typical stove, which is fashioned out of scrap metal — often recycled oil drums — by a multitude of neighborhood ironsmiths who know the requirements of their customers well and provide useful innovations within their customers' financial means.

In the rural areas, the market is many times bigger but much less affluent. Rural stoves, also made very inexpensively from local materials, often by the users themselves, also seem impervious to Western techniques of market research and mass marketing. Despite the absence of a commercial market, successful stove designs have being introduced by way of non-profitable innovations geared to local users. The following excerpt from the information service of the Centre for Science and Environment in New Delhi, India, an independent research institute, describes the combination of technical skills and market sensitivity required for innovations to occur.[4] The innovator is Madhu Sarin, a female Indian architect who became personally involved in the affairs of a village and its need for an improved stove, which they call a "chulha".

> Where scientists have failed, the dedicated tinkering of an architect in a Harijan (untouchable's) hamlet, Nada, situated at the foot of the Himalayan Shivalik hills, 15 km from Chandigarh, appears to be succeeding. The Nada chulha is a modification of the conventional chulha in the village, and this is probably one of the major reasons for its success.
>
> When Ms Madhu Sarin, the architect, first happened to visit Nada in 1980 she found a village woman Sheela, literally in tears from the smoke of her chulha. The thick black soot was on every

wall, ceiling and other household items. Sheela had tried to build another chulha against the wall but it too had not controlled the smoke.

The traditional chulha in Nada accommodates two pots.... The flow of hot air is not well controlled within the chulha and substantial quantities of heat are lost to the atmosphere. To improve the efficiency of a chulha it is important to control the flow of air which, in turn, controls the rate at which the fuel burns. A chimney helps to control the flow of air, which also takes the smoke out of the house.

Ms Sarin read the limited literature available and with the help of Sheela developed a new chulha similar to the older one.... The new Nada chulha has a chimney and between the chulha and the chimney there is a damper to control the flow of air. When fire is lighted, the air becomes hot and goes out of the only outlet, the chimney, as the entrance is partially closed by another damper made from an asbestos sheet. The two pots fit well into their seats so no heat is lost from around the pot....

The women now have a smokeless kitchen. Many of them have given a fresh paint of mud to their kitchen walls and have decorated their chulhas with traditional designs. They can now even take a hot-water bath and morning tea in winters from the water boiled in the second pot. The best thing about the new chulha, according to the village women, is that it works the moment the fire is lit.

What the women, who do the cooking, wanted most was

a smokefree environment, and that was what Sarin provided in the new stove she designed with the help of Sheela, the villager.

Removing waste heat from the kitchen also pleased the village women because their huts were less stuffy. Their kitchens had been so unbearable, particularly in summer, that they often cooked outside on an open fire, which consumed even more woodfuel than their traditional stove. As a by-product of their smokeless and less stuffy kitchens, much less wood is consumed:

> Villagers now collect firewood only once a week rather than twice a week. Firewood is the main fuel used by the villagers who average six hours trek each to collect it. The new chulha boils twelve litres of water while the old one boiled only seven litres with the same amount of wood. Five kilograms of firewood now last four full days.... It is quite possible that women in Nada have taken to the new chulha not because it is efficient but because it is smokeless, smoke being seen as a bigger problem by them than collecting firewood.

Sarin attributes her success to "understanding the villagers, their problems and perspectives .... unless one identifies with the people by helping to solve their problems, the villagers will not listen to any advice, leave alone working on it."

The Sarin stove has caught fire, and seems to be spreading to other parts of India, where attempts are being made to adapt it to local conditions. The 'experts' going into the communities are not men but "women volunteers .... women find it easier to communicate with the women."[5]

ASSUMING THAT PEOPLE act against their self-interest is rarely fruitful; more likely those doing the assuming simply do not understand what constitutes the self-interest of others, in the same way our Western experts did not realize that smoke control, and a less stuffy kitchen, mattered more to village women than fetching fuelwood.

Yet the Western view of the Third World is fraught with such assumptions, that the West not only knows what the Third World's problems are, but also knows how best to solve them. The toughest lesson we may have to learn is that our calculation of their problems may not coincide with their own calculations, that there may be very little for us to teach those in societies so different from ours, and that the best contribution we can make to the Third World's problems may be not so much in what we do for them, but in what we stop doing to them.

# CONCLUSIONS

# Toward Empowerment

# 17

# *These Are No Myths*

**"Business is business and human rights is human rights."**
**— Ross Campbell, then Chairman of Atomic Energy of Canada Ltd., in a 1978 meeting with the No Candu for Argentina Committee, Ottawa.**

IN THE NAME OF PROGRESS tribal people in Brazil's Amazon are being thrown off their land to provide cattle with grazing pastures, Haitian peasants are being dispossessed to make way for hydro dams that will provide power for multinational manufacturing companies, Tamil lands in Sri Lanka are being irrigated so they can be settled by the majority Sinhalese, and peasants in India are losing their traditional forests to the commercial interests of the national government. Rather than being exceptions, these projects are, in fact, the rule throughout the Third World, their victims sacrificial lambs offered to the god of progress in grand designs to develop the "underdeveloped" Third World. But the god is a false one, the progress illusory, and the grand designs only undermine the often precarious ability of the average Third World person to provide for himself.

Implicit in all of the projects that form the grand designs is a decision that a few must suffer for the greater national good, that this national good justifies even the violation of human rights. We in the Western countries cannot absolve ourselves of the responsibility for these misdeeds: our leaders not only tolerate but defend providing the financing which makes such projects possible. Marc Lalonde, as Canada's Minister of Finance and Governor of the World Bank, argued that an undemocratic government, even one with a deplorable human rights record, should not be denied funds by his bank or others like it:

> Virtually all contributors to these institutions .... have taken the view that the Bank can only function effectively by using technical and economic criteria as the sole standards for project and program approval. For this reason, we have resisted efforts which have been used from time to time by others to introduce other considerations, such as human rights, into [our] deliberations.[1]

These views, expressed by the public's representatives,

surely do not represent those of the public: progress in the West is not condoned if it comes at the expense of human rights. The same standards of decency that we demand at home should be applied abroad.

We can try to insure that the misdeeds which have occurred in the past do not recur in future by recognizing that many of the aspirations of people in the Third World are no different from ours: they want to be free from those who would abuse their rights, and free to pursue their own goals. We can best help them by rejecting the argument that it would be "cultural imperialism" for us to require that foreign aid projects do not violate human rights, that public reviews of the projects are held, and that information about projects is accessible. These conditions do nothing more than attempt to insure that foreign aid, which is by definition humanitarian, accomplishes its purpose. All other conditions attached to foreign aid — those designed to accomplish non-humanitarian purposes — are irrelevant to its purpose and should be detached from it.

Until we incorporate into our foreign aid programs the standards and principles of fairness that are expected to govern the use of public funds at home, we will not only be acting hypocritically. We will also be accomplices in violating the human rights of those we try hardest to help.

These principles should apply no less to our commercial export-development agencies, which also employ public funds — agencies like the Export-Import Bank in the U.S. and the Export Development Corporation in Canada. Although their foreign activities are less publicized than those of the foreign aid agencies, they provide comparable levels of funding for projects, and can do comparable amounts of damage.[2]

Apart from setting our own house in order, we can also

recognize that the people of the Third World have a right to self-determination, and that they understand, better than any foreign experts and better than their own governments, the environmental limits of the resources available to them, how to use those resources best, and the future they want for themselves.

## RECOMMENDATIONS

### Establish National Inquiries Into the Merits of Foreign Aid

After three decades of foreign aid, critics from many countries, of all ideological stripes and from many disciplines, have come to the conclusion that foreign aid is not working and that the problem may be fundamental — that foreign aid may be inherently debilitating rather than strengthening to the recipient.

Peter Bauer, considered by the *Wall Street Journal* "the world's foremost authority on economic development," says that aid "enables governments to pursue policies which patently retard growth and exacerbate poverty" while increasing the power of governments to behave in oppressive and murderous ways.[3] His thesis is that foreign aid and development planning have thoroughly politicized economic life through detailed government monopolization of the economy, with the result that acquiring political power has become all-important: "Not only the economic but even the physical survival of large numbers of people have come to depend on political and administrative decisions. Productive ethnic minorities have become conspicuous among victims."[4]

Bauer's conclusion, that aid is the problem, not the

solution, and that "the donor governments cannot wash their hands of the consequences of their so-called caring," is echoed by Cheryl Payer, author of *The World Bank*,[5] a highly critical analysis which argues the Third World would be better off if the World Bank went out of business. A critic of Western imperialism who condemns foreign aid for its "pernicious role" in militarily unstable regions like El Salvador, Payer nevertheless considers "these cases .... only the tip of the iceberg; even the 'normal' operations of foreign aid programs are functioning to hold back progressive development, not to finance it."

To these unequivocal condemnations of the use of foreign aid for development, which base much of their rationale on foreign aid's political flaws, is added Jane Jacobs' apolitical but equally uncompromising conclusion in *Cities and the Wealth of Nations* that "development cannot be given: it must be *done*."[6] Jacobs, who has been one of the world's most respected thinkers since her theories in the 1960s transformed the public's view of the way cities work, argues that foreign aid, by definition, cannot help develop an economy because development "is a process, not a collection of capital goods.... [The] loans, grants and subsidies sent into regions lacking vigorous cities can shape inert, unbalanced or permanently dependent regions, but are useless for creating self-generating economies.... The failure is built into the fact that they *are* loans, grants and subsidies; those golden eggs, being only gold, don't hatch goslings."

Our own research, which has concentrated on energy and energy-related issues, provides us with no solace that the other, more general criticisms, are not valid. The problem with energy aid, we have found, stems from the absence of an accountable and democratic process — an absence that starts in the Western donor countries and carries right through to the Third World recipients. This absence is not limited to energy projects, but occurs across the board. Foreign aid may not be salvageable, but if it is, we believe that a fundamental change in the process that governs it is a prerequisite.

Although inquiries into foreign aid and related issues have taken place over the years, they have been concerned with the means of improving aid: none have started by questioning the very premise that any or all forms of aid are beneficial.

This premise will not be an easy one for us to question. Charity and compassion for those less well off than ourselves are universal human instincts, and few are callous to the suffering and hardship that exist in the world.

But foreign aid has become a $25-billion-a-year business and warrants a public examination, as difficult as it may be on our emotions to examine the effects of our generosity. Should this inquiry determine that any or all forms of foreign aid are counter-productive, as some have claimed, the energies expended there can be channeled to finding other, more promising avenues for helping the Third World's poor. On the other hand, should foreign aid be found beneficial, the public will have renewed confidence in the expenditure of its tax dollars, and the foreign aid establishment will receive a second wind to relieve the "aid fatigue" it now complains of. We recommend that the terms of reference of the National Inquiry be:

> To determine whether foreign aid, in any of its manifestations, has been beneficial to its recipients, what the reasons have been for the successes or failures of foreign aid, and what the prospects are for foreign aid in the future.

This inquiry should be comprehensive. Distinctions should be made between projects which hold out the promise of developing a country, such as the hydro dams and other infrastructure projects that this book has been concerned with, and those that are more akin to charity, intended to further philanthropic purposes or relieve emergencies: clothing and shelter for earthquake victims, food for hungry children.

The process by which aid is administered should be evaluated to determine who is making the decisions, who should be making them, and on which bases. In the case of large capital projects like hydro dams, the enormous potential for good also carries with it an equally enormous potential for harm when the wrong dam is put in the wrong place because of an inadequate process of evaluation and selection.

Distinctions should also be made between the various delivery mechanisms for aid, because some may succeed where others fail.

Aid, and subsidies tantamount to aid, are delivered by financial bodies like the International Monetary Fund, a consortium of countries that provides credit to otherwise uncreditworthy countries; by multilateral development agencies like the World Bank, another consortium which mostly funds large development projects; by the agencies of individual countries, like the Canadian International Development Agency and the Agency for International Development; and by private voluntary organizations, like the Red Cross, Foster Parents Plan, and Oxfam, which also can undertake both development projects and charitable works, although generally on a much smaller scale.

The inquiry should assure its independence by having as its jurors individuals who have neither worked for the aid establishment nor taken previous public positions on foreign aid. It should fund intervenors from all walks of life, hear the views of expert witnesses from Western and Third World countries, and most importantly, it should hear the views of the people in the Third World who are affected by foreign aid projects.

A national inquiry, however, is not needed to prove that at least some foreign aid projects are detrimental to the Third World's poor; these failings can be remedied, in whole or in part, by undertaking the following interim measures immediately:

## Refuse Funding to Foreign Aid Projects That Violate the International Bill of Human Rights

Foreign aid, which is by definition humanitarian, cannot, by definition, countenance any violation of human rights. Although most Western countries have ratified the covenants of the International Bill of Human Rights,[7] and have thereby committed themselves to protect the wide range of human rights of their people, when it comes to the expenditure of their aid budgets in another country they reject this same commitment.

To insure that development projects do not adversely affect aid recipients, those who make development choices must be accountable for their environmental, social, and financial repercussions. This accountability requires that those who must live with the consequences of a project have ultimate control over it.

When a community's culture or livelihood is dependent on the physical environment that would be affected by an aid project, we recommend that all Western governments and their aid agencies:

1. refuse financial support for projects that are officially opposed by an indigenous group in accordance with its own governing processes.
2. refuse financial support for any projects that have any adverse impact on local populations unless the affected groups consent through internationally supervised negotiations.
3. refuse financial support to projects that require people to be relocated without their consent. When consent is given, compensation should be paid promptly and at a level agreed to by both parties.

For all communities, we recommend that Western governments and their aid agencies:

4. determine whether a project should proceed in a required public hearing process that includes:
   (a) full public disclosure of information about the projects in the countries giving the aid and in the country receiving the aid. This information should be available in the languages of all the populations involved.
   (b) a means to insure that the views of all people to be affected by a project are heard.
   (c) a full assessment of a project, complete with an assessment of the environmental and social cost of the project, paying special attention to the human and economic costs of relocating people.
   (d) the means whereby project proponents can be challenged on the very need for the project, as well as its environmental and social effects.

5. refuse financial support to any project in which a violation of human rights cannot be avoided.
6. withdraw funding from multilateral aid institutions that support projects that violate human rights.

In addition, to avoid similar mistakes in future, environmental, social, and economic evaluations should be conducted after current and future projects are completed and functioning.

## Refuse Cash Grants to Governments That Violate the International Bill of Rights

To insure that foreign aid in the form of cash for the general use of a government is not used to violate human rights, we recommend that Western governments and their aid agencies:

1. refuse to grant financial support to governments that do not respect the land rights of peasants, or the territorial sovereignty of indigenous peoples, in accordance with the International Bill of Human Rights, which stipulates that peoples shall determine their own political status and be free to pursue their economic, social and cultural development.[8]
2. withdraw financial support from those governments that attempt to destroy traditional lifestyles or to force the acculturation, assimilation, or destruction of indigenous peoples.
3. refuse to grant financial support to governments whose treatment of their own people is abhorrent to the citizens of the aid-giving country.[9]

## Refuse Government Subsidies to Western Companies That Violate Human Rights in the Third World

Western companies which sell to Third World countries should not have access to taxpayers' funds if companies' projects are abhorrent to taxpayers, as are violations of human rights abroad. The capital projects funded by government export agencies like the Export Development Corporation and the Export-Import Bank should be subject to the same public review process that applies to foreign aid funded projects. Because very few Western corporations participate in Third World projects that do not have some form of financial support from Western Governments, either in the form of foreign aid or export promotion subsidies supporting them, the effect of this recommendation would be to bring virtually all major capital projects which are financed by Westerners under public scrutiny at home and in the Third World.

## Use Foreign Aid Solely to Benefit the Recipient Peoples, Not to Further the Donor's Commercial Goals

To promote exports, Western governments currently provide their exporters with a raft of incentives, including loans and grants in case they need financing, insurance in case their customers are unable to pay their bills, research and development subsidies, travel expenses, and insurance against the imposition of extraordinary foreign regulations which interfere with their business. As well, our governments provide potential Third World importers of our goods and services with incentives, such as low-interest loans and extended repayment plans with which to make the purchase.

Our governments also facilitate sales by creating departments for trade promotion, sending our political leaders abroad to create a good business climate, and turning parts of their embassies into sales offices. If governments feel more export assistance is required, they should increase funding through existing or new channels designed for this purpose. They should not compromise foreign aid by requiring it to serve business masters at home, through the tying of foreign aid.

In any case, the tying of a project's aid to the purchase of goods and services from the donor country only benefits a handful of producers, is largely irrelevant to the national economy of the donor, and is likely to force the recipient Third World country into making second-best or counterproductive purchases. We therefore recommend that the recipients of foreign aid be free to purchase goods and services of their choice from any suppliers anywhere in the world, on the condition that the purposes for which they are intended are acceptable to the donor.[10]

## Use Foreign Aid Solely to Benefit the Recipient Peoples, Not to Further Domestic or Foreign Policy Goals of the Donor Government

Western taxpayers give foreign aid to help people in poorer countries, not to help their own government. But Western governments often use the funds they collect from taxpayers to further specific political goals. The U.S. has been accused of appropriating foreign aid funds to shore up the governments of some Central American countries because they are strategic militarily, and Canada has been accused of disbursing foreign aid to the French speaking countries in Africa, in part to preempt the province of Quebec, which had been trying to legitimize its goal of sovereignty by establishing relations with French speaking countries.[11]

Using foreign aid for any purpose other than to further strict humanitarian purposes, whether the purpose is political, military, or commercial, discredits the institution of foreign aid. These non-humanitarian purposes should be furthered through appropriate channels, and bilateral aid should be stripped of its government partisanship.

As an interim measure, this can be accomplished by a cabinet directive to the foreign aid agencies of our governments. But other means of depoliticizing foreign aid are possible, which the national inquiries into foreign aid should consider. As an example, taxpayers could be given the right to pick the countries to which their foreign aid contribution can go, should they so choose, instead of having the federal government do so.

This direction by taxpayers could be made on their income tax returns through a simple form like the following:

> Please direct the foreign aid portion of my income tax to the following countries in the following proportions. Send:
>
> ....... percent of my foreign aid to .......
> ....... percent of my foreign aid to .......
> ....... percent of my foreign aid to .......
>
> Please direct (the balance, if any)(all) of my foreign aid to the citizens of those countries which you think require it most. But please exclude the following countries:
>
> .................. ..................
> .................. ..................

This form provides an illustration of how a government's motives in distributing foreign aid can be defused. The role of the federal government would shift from that of a proponent to that of an administrator of foreign aid funds, first setting the total amount to be disbursed and then insuring that the funds voted to a country by taxpayers are disbursed in a manner that does not violate human rights, that provides for a fair public process, and that lends itself to auditing. Because the funds would be untied, the foreign aid bureaucracy would play a smaller role than at present: the responsibility for choosing a project and seeing to its completion would shift to the Third World from the Western aid agencies, who would no longer need to retain technical experts on every country and on every type of development project. The projects which would be funded under these recommendations would also tend to be smaller than at present, because the aid agencies could not commit public funds into the future. The funds allocated to a country in any one year could be spread out over several years, or used all at once on a project, but they could not all be spent in the first year of a multi-year project on the expectation that the public would direct more to that particular country in the following years. This bias away from megaprojects is likely to reduce the chance that megamistakes will be made.

The federal government would still have some discretionary funds to allocate to projects it wanted to support by virtue of the amount that taxpayers had allotted to its discretion, but it would also tend to be more cautious with these funds, because their misallocation would likely lead to fewer taxpayers trusting the federal government's judgment in future.

The public in the West would likely view foreign aid very differently under this system. No taxpayers would need to feel disgruntled that their tax dollars were supporting a regime they disliked, and all taxpayers would likely be more interested and more committed to where their tax dollars were going. The federal government would publish which countries were receiving how much money, sparking a debate about whether the neediest countries were getting enough, or the less needy were getting too much. As the public was convinced of one or another point of view, funds would slowly shift from some countries to others. All countries, no doubt, would have their champions, who would also keep Third World issues at the forefront.

## Increase the Role of Privately Funded Charitable Groups Aiding the Third World

If any type of foreign aid is likely to be found beneficial by the national inquiry and unlikely to be found to cause harm, it is the small projects developed by churches and private Western charitable organizations like Oxfam that work directly with their counterparts in Third World countries. Tax mechanisms to encourage public support of their projects should be adopted as an interim measure, pending the results of the inquiry. Donors to these charitable organizations should receive tax credits for their donations instead of the tax deductions currently used. These tax credits would give less affluent donors the same tax benefit as affluent ones as well as providing a greater incentive to provide help.[12] Charities that receive government funds to carry out their projects — as is the case, to a large extent, in Canada — would also be subject to those safeguards against human rights abuses outlined earlier in this chapter.

## Adopt Neutral Policies Regarding Technologies the West Should Promote to the Third World

No technology should be promoted to the exclusion of others. This recommendation, for even-handed policies, may be the hardest of all for us to accept. Although some of us may view all Western technology as superior, and others may prefer some technologies in particular, such as solar and other renewable energy technologies, how and where technological change is best introduced depends on a host of local factors and local needs. Local people are the best judge of these, and should be the ultimate decisionmakers.

# Acknowledgements

WE ARE GRATEFUL to those who have helped shape this book with their advice and careful comments on the text: Marilyn Aarons, Vicki Berry, Margaret Biggs, Howard Daugherty, Jenny Fraser, Hinda Goldberg, Moira Hutchinson, Florentine Krause, David MacDonald, Linda Marshall, Francesca Patterson, David Poch, Norman Rubin, Kate Sutherland, and Philip Williams.

We are also grateful to those who have so diligently contributed in other capacities. For their research on our behalf: Charles Drucker, Angela Gennino, and Jamie Lee. For typing the many drafts of the manuscript: Kathleen Brown, Joan Burke, Georges Gagnon, Brit Griffin, Marco Lam, Kate Revington, Natty Urquizo, and Hamish Wilson. For the artistic production of the book: Gene Threndyle.

And, finally, for the otherwise thankless task of compiling the index, thanks to Barbara Tschannen and Marg Pilger.

Less thankful are we to the printer's devils that we will blame for any typographical errors that have crept into the text, and for our own failure to catch more serious errors that may remain.

The various observations, opinions, and expressions of political philosophy are also our own.

# Notes

**N.B.** Currencies are stated in local dollars for the U.S. and Canada. For all other countries, U.S. dollars apply.

*Preface*, pages 10-15

1. Our letters to officials at CIDA, the Department of External Affairs, and the multilateral development banks date back to early 1983. In March 1983 we sent CIDA a copy of a study that showed how two Haitian hydrodams being considered for funding by the Inter-American Development Bank (of which Canada is a member) would displace thousands of small farmers, undermine Haiti's ability to feed itself, and increase the number of unemployed. We asked for their position on these claims and in January 1984 received the following statement from William McWhinney, Senior Vice-President: "I must inform you that it is not CIDA policy to comment on projects which are not our own." This statement was made despite the fact that CIDA coordinates Canada's participation in the IDB. Officials at the Inter-American Development Bank itself also refused to comment.

In another letter, dated January 23, 1984, the Secretary of State for External Affairs, Allan MacEachen, claimed that "Canada did not help build the large Akosomobo Dam in Ghana some 20 years ago," although CIDA announced in a press release dated August 25, 1969 that their $5,830,000 loan for the provision of electrical generators, and ancillary equipment for the Volta River power station at Akosombo "will complete the Volta River project."

On the other hand, MacEachen was quick to point out that "Canada was responsible for the highly successful K'pong dam in Ghana, whose well managed, small-scale resettlement project is often cited by authorities as a demonstration of how this should be done." However, requests by us for details of this project and for details of other successful hydro projects, made to CIDA in May 1984, have so far gone unanswered.

In still another letter of March 29, 1984, we asked William McWhinney at CIDA for details of the Kompienga hydro project in Upper Volta which was expected to produce power at more than twice the normal cost ($8000 per kw) and for which there was no environmental assessment, despite the fact that it was being built in a game park. At the time of publication of this book still no answer to this request had been received.

The assumption that hydroelectric dams must be, on balance, beneficial is evident in MacEachen's January 23, 1984 letter: "However, hydro projects, as well as providing the energy benefits to which we can all attest in Canada, often provide side benefits on a huge scale," (in chapter 2 we discuss in detail the general benefits he cites).

2. It was with shock that we discovered, while researching this book and in the course of trying to obtain information on damaging projects, how secretive aid officials are about their activities in the Third World: some questions are simply never answered (see note 1), those that are answered usually take months to arrive, and as was explained by officials at the IDB and CIDA (see IDB letter of May 25, 1983 from the Canadian Executive Director's office to Energy Probe and the CIDA letter of January 3, 1984 from W. McWhinney to Energy Probe), feasibility studies and environmental assessments for projects funded by these agencies are the property of the country receiving the aid. Therefore, the public that finances these projects cannot see the basis on which decisions are made to fund them. And if the Third World country chooses not to release information about these projects to citizens of Western countries or to its own citizens (which is often the case as we explain in chapters 1 and 10), then it is virtually impossible for the people

who ultimately finance the projects and those who must live with their consequences to get even the most basic details about them.

Virtually no one can get internal multilateral bank documents because they are highly restricted. To overcome this secrecy, the U.S. Congress began attaching, in the 1970s, a provision in each year's Appropriation Act requiring that these documents be available to members of the U.S. government. However, before they can be released to members of the U.S. public, if the bank is willing to release them at all, they must be edited by the bank and the U.S. Treasury Department.

Not only are these aid agencies secretive, they are also unaccountable. With respect to international multilateral agencies such as the World Bank, their staff cannot be subpoenaed to appear before legislative bodies. In the U.S., for example, because the multilateral banks are exempt from appearing before any legislative body, they deal with Congress solely through the Treasury Department.

Each country is represented at the bank by a Governor, which in Canada's case is either the Secretary of State for External Affairs (for the four regional development banks) or the Minister of Finance (for the World Bank and the IMF). This was intended to be a mechanism for accountability. However, statements such as that made by the Secretary of State for External Affairs (and by the senior Vice-President of CIDA — see note 1) that the IDB, not Canada, was funding a feasibility study of a hydroelectric dam in Haiti, indicate the mechanism is not working. If Canada's Governor to the IDB does not accept responsibility on behalf of Canada for the IDB's foreign aid projects, then who will? The ambiguity of responsibility for the activities of these multilateral aid agencies, and the willingness of our representatives to disown the banks when they are bad, casts doubt on the wisdom of remaining in them as members.

*Introduction*, pages 16-23

1. "Philippines faces economic collapse," in Report on Business, *Globe and Mail*, September 27, 1984. Also see "The Revolt Within" by T.D. Allman in *Harper's*, September 1984.

2. Cranford Pratt's book, *The Critical Phase in Tanzania 1945-1968: Nyerere and the Emergence of A Socialist Strategy*, Cambridge University Press, 1976, illustrates Tanzania's search for institutional forms of mass participation and democratic control which would be expressive of communal values within a one-party state. About the 1963 to 1967 period he concludes: "Whatever the longer-term democratic potential of the new structures .... their immediate consequences have been to consolidate power in the hands of the present leaders, to silence their critics and to lessen the autonomy of previously independent institutions."

Despite President Nyerere's conviction that "A people cannot be developed: they can only develop themselves," that people cannot be coerced into a socialist society, he insisted on using pressure to get the peasants to live in villages. Fearing that Tanzania would develop slowly as long as peasants lived in their scattered homesteads, in 1967 he set forth the principles of "ujamaa" — people living and working together for the good of all in democratic communities. Initially, the purpose was to consolidate rural communities into villages, enabling the provision of local services such as schools, water supplies, agricultural and veterinary services, and political education. Later, peasants were urged not only to live in villages but also to farm communally. While he allowed the implementation of the latter policy to lag, Pratt explains that Nyerere felt villagization was "such a basic requirement of progress that some coercion may be justified to overcome initial opposition to it."

3. From "Beyond Africa's present crisis," by John Madeley in *New Scientist*, August 2, 1984. John Madeley gives, as one of the reasons for this unexpected outcome, the fact that women and children are exploited by men who want to market their produce in order to have money for beer and other luxuries. "When the national economy is in a mess, there is less opportunity for that exploitation."

4. *ibid.*

5. Although foreign aid accounts for only about 35 percent of total flows of financial resources to developing countries (see *OECD Development Co-operation: 1982 Review*, OECD, Paris, 1982), it is extremely influential because other sources of funding for

development projects (which are often too large and too risky to be funded by any one source) come forth once a project receives a commitment from a foreign aid agency. Joint financing of many development projects comes from national aid agencies, multilateral aid agencies (such as the World Bank), export promotion agencies of Western countries, commercial banks, and by the recipient Third World governments themselves. These development projects are more likely to be backed by non-aid sources if they fit into a grand development scheme (Five and Ten Year Plans) usually prepared at the behest of the aid agencies who want to see how the aid they are giving will fit into the jigsaw puzzle of an emerging Third World industrial economy. For these reasons, the bilateral aid agencies that channel country-to-country aid, and the multilateral aid agencies that channel the pooled aid funds from many industrial countries to Third World countries, have great influence over the setting of Third World development agendas.

6. "Lending Institutions Stall Latin American Progress," by Manuel F. Ayau in the *Wall Street Journal*, November 18, 1983, also describes how spending by these international agencies has undermined the national welfare, by:

> putting governments in the business of power generation and distribution, telecommunications, railroads, shipping or other ventures that invariably end up charging monopoly prices and losing money to boot....
>
> A typical case: During the last two decades, the government of Guatemala socialized the electricity business. Over these years, several small, uneconomical hydro and thermal plants have been built by the government, and recently a very large hydro plant was completed. The political changes in Guatemala have not resulted in stable and sound planning or operating procedures. The end result is that individuals and industry are now paying more than 12 cents a kilowatt-hour, four times the competitive rate.
>
> The problem is aggravated by lending institutions that insist that electric power rates guarantee a 9 percent yield on capital investment in order to service the debt. Of course, the soundness of such a policy is not considered. (It's a bit

like the child who is selling lemonade at $1,000 a glass; all she has to do is sell one glass.)

Because it is illegal to generate power for sale, many firms have opted to purchase diesel engines to produce their own power at a cost of eight cents a kwh. It is also cheaper to cook with imported propane than with the existing hydro-generated power. These uneconomical expenditures on diesel engines, diesel fuel, propane and other fuels would not be necessary were it not for the government's energy venture. The overall effect is to drain the Guatemalan economy by making local industry noncompetitive with foreign producers and to cause severe economic strain for the average Guatemalan energy-user.

7. Energy development projects in the Third World over the last three decades have focussed almost exclusively on the production of electrical power. Only recently have aid agencies begun to show interest in the development of oil and gas and new energy sources such as geothermal energy and renewable energy. Cheryl Payer in her book, *The World Bank: A Critical Analysis*, Monthly Review Press, New York, 1982, reports: "The financing of electric power projects was one of the first types of lending from the World Bank to Third World nations; and for many years it remained the largest sector. At the end of fiscal year 1980 it represented, cumulatively, the second largest sector, after agriculture and rural development, with over $14 billion, or 21 percent of the total funds lent by the Bank for all purposes throughout its history."

The other multilateral development banks dedicated roughly the same proportion of their total lending to energy as did the World Bank: 23 percent for the Asian Development Bank between 1972 and 1978; 25 percent for the Inter-American Development Bank between 1972 and 1978. And, like the World Bank, the vast majority of their energy loans went to electric power. In those periods the Asian Development Bank loaned 98.3 percent to electricity generation and transmission and the Inter-American Development Bank loaned 94.1 percent to electricity generation and transmission. Well over half of these loans went to the generation and transmission of hydroelectricity. For more details on this see, *The World Energy Triangle*, by Thomas Hoffman and Brian

Johnson, Ballinger Publishing Company, Massachusetts, 1981. Also see note 2, chapter 3.

8. This is not to say that people in infertile valleys or plains cannot be agriculturally successful. The South African bushmen are a good example of a people who have adapted their techniques of subsistence to what is, by most measures, an inhospitable, harsh, and barren physical environment. However, the river valleys in the Third World that are potential sites for hydroelectric development are usually populated by farming communities who have settled there to take advantage of the natural fertilization and irrigation provided by the annual floods, or to take advantage of the water supply for their man-made irrigation systems. In Nigeria, 50,000 people who lived along the Niger river and who used it for irrigation and small commercial fishing were forced to move to less fertile upland soil by the World Bank- and CIDA-sponsored Kainji Dam.

9. From brochures describing the work of the Anti-Slavery Society today. The Anti-Slavery Society for the Protection of Human Rights is located in London, England.

10. One example of a jointly financed megaproject is the Brazilian Tucurui hydroelectric plant (part of the Tocantins River Basin Hydroelectric Project). Providing a portion of the loans to cover its $4 billion price tag are: the Arab Banking Corporation, Bank of America, Canadian Imperial Bank of Commerce, Chase Merchant Banking Group, Dresdner Bank A.G., Libra Bank Ltd., National Bank of Canada and Nippon Credit Corporation. Reported in the *Brazil-Canada Newsletter*, July/August 1981, published by the Brazil-Canada Chamber of Commerce, Toronto. The power from the dam is intended for aluminum plants and the Great Carajas project — a $62 billion program of mining, forestry and agricultural development in the Brazilian Amazon region, which is in part being funded by the World Bank. The dam — the world's fourth largesopment in the Brazilian Amazon region, which is in part being funded by the World Bank. The dam — the world's fourth largest — will produce 8,000 MW, create a 834 square mile reservoir where tropical forests once stood, necessitate the resettlement of as many as 30,000 non-Amerindian people, and flood the lands (or cover the land with transmission lines) belonging to some

87,000 indigenous people including the Parakanan, Surui, Gavioes, Guajajara/Tenethehara, Amanaye, Anambe, and Assurini Indians. For more information on Tucurui see *Environmental Assessment of the Tucurui Hydroproject Rio Tocantins, Amazonia, Brazil*, by Robert Goodland, 1978 Eletronorte S/A, Brazil, and for the effect of Tucurui and the Great Carajas Program on the indigenous people see *The Global Reporter*, The Anthropology Resource Center, March 1983; *Indian Areas Threatened by Hydroelectric Projects in Brazil*, by Paul L. Aspelin and Silvio Coelho dos Santos, International Work Group for Indigenous Affairs Document 44, Copenhagen, October 1981; and, "Electric Colonialism," by Paul L. Aspelin in *Soft Energy Notes*, San Francisco, July/August 1982.

11. "A Third World Spring?" by Flora Lewis in the *New York Times*, April 8, 1984.
12. *ibid.*
13. *ibid.*
14. "Central American Aid — A Waste," by Walter LaFeber in the *New York Times*, February 26, 1984.
15. "A Third World Spring?" *op. cit.*

*Chapter 1*, pages 27-36

1. The *International Bill of Human Rights*, including the Universal Declaration of Human Rights, the International Covenant on Economic, Social and Cultural Rights, and the International Covenant on Civil and Political Rights and the Optional Protocol to the International Covenant on Civil and Political Rights, published by the Office of Public Information, United Nations, New York 1978. The U.N. transformed the principles of the Universal Declaration of Human Rights (proclaimed by the U.N. General Assembly in 1948) into treaty provisions which establish legal obligations on the part of each ratifying State. These are enshrined in two covenants: the International Covenant on Economic, Social and Cultural Rights and the International Covenant on Civil and Political Rights. The Universal Declaration applies to "all peoples and all nations." Both covenants outline in their preambles "the inherent dignity .... the equal and inalienable rights of all members

of the human family." Both, although with slightly different wording, recognize "the ideal of free human beings enjoying freedom from fear and want can only be achieved if conditions are created whereby everyone may enjoy his economic, social and cultural rights, as well as his civil and political rights." In addition to these universal standards there are also the unequivocal rights as outlined in the International Labor Organization's Convention 107, "Convention Concerning the Protection and Integration of Indigenous and other Tribal and Semi-Tribal Populations in Independent Countries," which are referred to by groups like Survival International in their defense of indigenous peoples rights: "The right of ownership, collective or individual, of the members of the populations concerned over the lands which these populations traditionally occupy shall be recognized." See especially Article 11 in *Conventions and Recommendations Adopted By the International Labor Conference at its Fortieth Session*, International Labor Organization, Geneva, 1957.

2. This statement appears as part (ii) of Articles 1 in both the International Covenant on Economic, Social and Cultural Rights, and the International Covenant on Civil and Political Rights of the *International Bill of Human Rights*, *op. cit.*

3. Article 25 of the International Covenant on Economic, Social and Cultural Rights of the *International Bill of Human Rights*, *op. cit.*

4. Article 27 of the International Covenant on Civil and Political Rights of the *International Bill of Human Rights*, *op. cit.*

5. Of course, energy projects are not the only culprits. A whole gamut of projects, especially "frontier development" projects, deprive people of their land. For example, the controversial Polonoroeste Project to develop the mineral, forest and agricultural resources of an area larger than the state of California in North-west Brazil will endanger the lives and land of some 8,000 people comprising 30 different indigenous groups. This is being funded by the World Bank.

Moreover, it is not just aid money that funds these projects but also export promotion packages to industrial country consultants and manufacturers. For example, Canada's Export Development Corporation, which insures Canadian exporters against non-payment — generally "sweetening" export deals to help make Canadian exports more competitive — has facilitated Canadian corporate involvement in some notorious hydroelectric projects around the world. For example, $3.5 million in U.S. funds went to help a Brazilian electric utility purchase from Canadian General Electric and Dominion Engineering Works shunt reactors for Brazil and Paraquay's gargantuan Itaipu hydroelectric complex (which displaced 42,000 farmers without adequate compensation); $60.1 million in Canadian funds went to a Venezuelan electric utility to purchase generators, exciters, installation and technical services from Canadian General Electric for Guri II, a hydroelectric dam opposed by indigenous peoples. The dam, half-owned by Reynolds Metals, powers an aluminum smelter. This information came from correspondence from EDC (June 21, 1983) to Energy Probe.

6. *The Philippines: Authoritarian government, multinationals and ancestral lands* by the Anti-Slavery Society, Indigenous Peoples and Development series Report No. 1 — 1983, England.

7. After the 1980 killing of a Kalinga elder and spokesman by the Philippine Armed Forces, the World Bank withdrew its funding for the dams. However, it continued to fund the Chico River Irrigation Project (downstream of the dams project) which will operate at one-third capacity until the hydrodams, which provide necessary water storage, are built. Although the 1981 Philippine Five-year National Energy Program made no mention of the Chico Dams, residents of the valley fear that it has not been cancelled, but only postponed because power lines and irrigation canals that will feed off the Chico Dams have already begun to march across the neighboring lowland provinces. See "Dam the Chico: Hydropower Development and Tribal Resistance" by Charles Drucker, San Francisco, 1984 (to be published by *The Ecologist* in England).

Additional information on the Chico Dams comes from the following sources: *International Work Group for Indigenous Affairs Newsletter*, No. 34, Denmark, July 1983; *Anthropology Resource Center Newsletter*, March 1981; *Survival International Information Packs*, April 1983 and *Survival International Review*, Vol. 6, No. 3 (35) and Vol. 6, No. 4 (36); *Cultural Survival Newsletter*, Summer 1980.

8. *Dam the Chico, op. cit.*
9. *The Philippines: Authoritarian government, multinationals and ancestral lands, op. cit.*
10. ibid
11. ibid
12. *ARC Newsletter, op. cit.*
13. *The Philippine: Authoritarian government, multinationals and ancestral lands, op. cit.*
14. "Resettlement" by Thayer Scudder in *Man-made Lakes and Human Health* by N.F. Stanley and M.P. Alpers (editors), New York, Academic Press, 1975.
15. *The World Bank: A Critical Analysis* by Cheryl Payer, Monthly Review Press, New York, 1982.
16. Disease also increased in the areas bordering Lake Kariba, the artificial lake that was created. For example, bilharzia, a debilitating and sometimes fatal disease spread by a snail that thrives in calm waters, was spread dramatically by a water-weed that covered most of the surface of the lake in its first years. From *Large Dams and the Developing World: Social and Environmental Costs and Benefits — A Look at Africa* by Warren Linney and Susan Harrison, Environment Liaison Centre, Nairobi, Kenya, September 1981.
17. Another researcher, Eugene K. Balon, describes in "Kariba: The Dubious Benefits of Large Dams" in *Ambio*, Volume 7, No. 2, 1978, how the people of the Gwembe Valley (the valley flooded by Lake Kariba), who were once food self-sufficient, two decades later still depended on outside sources of food. "Only a small part of the human population along the shores of Lake Kariba is engaged in fishing, while the majority are farmers reaping a very meager harvest and suffering from frequent crop failures; most of the time they depend on government grain subsidies."
18. According to an internal World Bank document, between 1969 and 1978, 170,000 members of tribal groups were forced to move so that their lands could be flooded by bank-financed hydroelectric schemes. See *Tropical Moist Forests: The Resources, The People, The Threat* by Catherine Caufield, An Earthscan Paperback, 1982.
19. Human rights abuses on a large scale have taken place in the

past in Canada and the U.S. — our treatment of blacks and indigenous peoples the best known among them. But because our institutions have evolved to better protect minorities, the scale of abuse currently present in the West does not approach that found today in the Third World.

20. From a petition signed by 2,622 T'bolis of Lake Sebu in the Philippines to the Asian Development Bank published in *The Philippines: Authoritarian government, multinationals and ancestral lands, op. cit.*

*Chapter 2*, pages 37-44

1. The international development banks, such as the World Bank and the four regional development banks, lend 100 percent of their aid. Bilateral agencies provide both outright grants and loans. For example, Canada's bilateral aid agency, CIDA, lent 65 to 75 percent of its 1980-83 energy aid budget while the remaining 25 to 35 percent was given as grants. From Energy Probe correspondence with Peter Haines, Vice-President, Resources Branch, CIDA, January 17, 1984.

2. World Bank information sheet issued by their Public Relations Department, Washington, D.C. (no date given).

3. The original price for electricity from the Akosombo Dam, negotiated by Kaiser and Reynolds, was 2.625 mills and was to remain in force for thirty years. David Hart (see note 7) calculated that by 1976, despite a rise in the rate to 3.25 mills, Reynolds and Kaiser were not paying the cost price of generating the electricity it used. Researchers for the Washington-based Center for Development Policy and the Worldwatch Institute calculated that if 56 developing countries with over 100 hydroelectric plants raised their electricity rates to the world average they would gain $10 billion in new annual revenues. From: "Let the Price of Hydro Rise" by S. Biddle and D. Deudney in *Renews*, No. 9, Non-governmental Organization newspaper for the U.N. Conference on New and Renewable Sources of Energy, Nairobi, August 1981.

4. *The World Bank: A Critical Analysis*, by Cheryl Payer, Monthly Review Press, New York, 1982.

5. *Fortune*, October, 1975.

6. *Cities and the Wealth of Nations* by Jane Jacobs, Random House, New York, 1984.
127. *The Volta River Project: A Case Study in Politics and Technology* by David Hart. University Press, Edinburgh, 1980.
8. This expression of hope that the Volta River Project would turn Ghana into a Utopia was made by Grace Ayensu, a member of the Convention Peoples Party, in the *Legislative Assembly Debates*, February 22, 1961, Ghana. See David Hart's study (note 7) for this quote.
9. From a January 23, 1984 response by the Secretary of State for External Affairs, Allan J. MacEachen, to an Energy Probe newsletter addressing the costs of large-scale hydro dams in Third World countries.
10. Take, for example, the Cerron Grande hydroelectric project in El Salvador funded by the World Bank and the Inter-American Development Bank. Robert Goodland, at the time an ecologist with the Cary Arboretum of the New York Botanical Garden, Environmental Protection Program, noted in his environmental assessment of the project that "5 or 10 thousand people or more (it is frightening that construction can be permitted to start even before the number of people are known), live in the area to be flooded and will be forced to abandon their homes." See *Cerron Grande Hydroelectric Project: Environmental Impact Reconnaissance* by Robert Goodland for The World Bank, April, 1973. Apparently, no one ever traced where these evacuees ended up, but many were believed to have simply joined the ranks of the urban unemployed.
11. See note 3. The low price Ghana received for its power forced the scrapping of the plans originally agreed to by Ghana and Kaiser. These involved the establishment of an alumina processing plant to use Ghana's 400 million ton bauxite reserve (instead of importing bauxite for Kaiser's aluminum smelter). As Nicholas Burnett reports in *Multinational Monitor*, "Kaiser Shortcircuits Ghanaian Development," February 1980, Kaiser's payments to Ghana barely cover the interest and amortization payments on the $117 million in loans taken out to build the Akosombo Dam, let alone pay the $500 to $600 million for an alumina refinery. As the Chief Executive Officer of Kaiser's project put it, "Ghana can't afford these extra foreign exchange costs at present."

12. The *Globe and Mail*, Toronto, June 9, 1983, reported that because of lack of rain and low water conditions the Volta River Authority requested that Kaiser and Reynolds postpone operations of their smelter until hydroelectric generating conditions improved. A year later, still no power was being produced by either the Akosombo Dam or the K'pong Dam, 20 miles downstream. From Energy Probe correspondence with Ontario Hydro, June 27, 1984.
13. *The Volta River Project*, *op. cit.* The plan would have delivered irrigation water by gravity from Volta Lake and by pumping water from the Volta River to 440,000 acres of the Accra Plains south of the dam site. "Large-scale mechanized agricultural methods were to be used on plots that were all to be above a minimum size .... fertilizers and pesticides were to be liberally used." However, as Hart explains, "No moves have been made to implement this scheme so that the idea of irrigating the Accra Plains remains in abeyance."
14. *The State of India's Environment 1982 — A Citizens' Report*, The Centre for Science and Environment, New Delhi, 1982.
15. *ibid.*
16. *Desertification*, by Alan Grainger, An Earthscan Paperback, London, 1982.

As early as 1969 alarms were sounded about massive irrigation systems. Dr. Raymond L. Nace of the U.S. Geological Survey told a UNESCO conference in 1969 that farmers displaced by the Kariba Dam between Zambia and Zimbabwe (then Rhodesia) experienced one bumper crop on the new land, but since then farming has been dogged by a series of disasters resulting from unanticipated changes in the water table and water level and the new necessity of plowing in the rainy season. See "Water projects lack full studies on effects" in *The Kingston Whig-Standard*, Kingston, Canada, December 17, 1969.
17. M.K. Ranjitsinh writes in *Ambio* that "As countries turn more and more to hydropower to meet their energy requirements .... the populations that do have to be relocated are almost invariably settled on cleared forestland, that being almost the only arable land now left in most countries." See "Forest Destruction in Asia and the South Pacific," *Ambio*, Vol. 8, No.5, 1979. In the case of both

the Kainji Dam in Nigeria and the Kariba Dam between Zambia and Zimbabwe (then Rhodesia) — both funded by the World Bank — communities evacuated from the valleys to be flooded were settled on less fertile upland soils. See *Large Dams and the Developing World, Social and Environmental Costs and Benefits: A Look at Africa* by Warren Linney and Susan Harrison for the Environment Liaison Centre, Kenya, September 1981.

*Chapter 3*, pages 45-49

1. The two new sites, at La Chapelle and Verrettes on the Artibonite River, were identified in a Canadian aid-funded survey of Haiti's hydroelectric potential: *Potential hydro-electrique de la riviere Artibonite* by Lalonde, Girouard, Lentendre et Associés Ltée. Projet d'Inventaire des Ressources Hydrauliques, Agence Canadienne de Développement International, République d'Haiti, Juin 1976.
2. See Introduction, note 7. The power generation projects funded by the major aid agencies tended to favor hydroelectricity over thermal-generated electricity. In the last decade, the World Bank lent slightly more to hydroelectric than to thermal electric projects while the Asian Development Bank lent almost twice as much. All of the Inter-American Development Bank's power generation projects were for hydroelectricity, over 90 percent of the European Development Fund's power budget, close to half of the Federal Republic of Germany's, and 87 percent of Britain's. Since the late 1970s virtually 100 percent of CIDA's power generation budget has gone to hydroelectricity, and, in the latter half of the 1970s, 85 percent of France's power generation aid budget went to hydroelectricity. From *The World Energy Triangle: A Strategy for Cooperation* by Thomas Hoffman and Brian Johnson, International Institute for Environment and Development, Ballinger Publishing Company, Massachusetts, 1981.
3. *The Quest for Harmony* by Calestous Juma, published by the Environment Liaison Centre, Nairobi, August 1980.
4. *Large Dams and the Developing World: Social and Environmental Costs and Benefits: A Look at Africa.* by Warren Linney

and Susan Harrison, published by the Environment Liaison Centre, Nairobi, September 1981.
5. *Down to Earth: Environment and Human Needs* by Erik Eckholm, International Institute for Environment and Development, Pluto Press, Great Britain, 1982.
6. *The State of India's Environment 1982: A Citizens' Report* by the Centre for Science and Environment, New Delhi, 1982. This is an excellent source of information on watershed management programs and their effect on the rural population. See also the testimony of Brent Blackwelder, Director of the Water Resources Policy Project at the Environmental Policy Institute, in the transcripts of the U.S. House of Representatives Committee on Banking, Finance and Urban Affairs, Subcommittee on International Development Institutions and Finance, *Environmental Impact of Multilateral Development Bank-funded Projects*, June 28 and 29, Washington, 1983.
7. Brent Blackwelder's testimony, *op. cit.*
8. See *Not Man Apart*, October 1983, published by Friends of the Earth, San Francisco, for their collection of articles entitled "Damming the World."
9. "Muddy waters move mountains" by D.E. Walling in *The Geographical Magazine*, May 1984.
10. *ibid.*
11. Some researchers have placed an economic value on this loss of topsoil through erosion. In his article, "Sedimentation problems in river basins" in *Nature and Resources*, UNESCO, April-June 1983, Ake Sundborg quotes a Swedish International Development Agency study that estimated that during the 1970s in Kenya soil erosion accounted each year for an economic loss that was higher than the value of the annual gross national product.
12. "Science losing malaria fight to mosquitoes" in *Globe and Mail*, October 11, 1983.
13. *ibid.* See also *The Quest for Harmony*, *op. cit.*
14. Brent Blackwelder's testimony, *op. cit.*
15. See note 2. Also, in the Memorandum of Canada to the Development Assistance Committee of the Organization for Economic Co-operation and Development, *Annual Aid Review 1982*, Canadian aid officials describe the dimensions of the 1982

energy aid program as being an "emphasis on smaller-scale energy technologies to complement Canada's traditional and continuing focus on major hydroelectric generation and distribution projects."

*Chapter 4*, pages 50-57

1. *The Economic Effects of an Untying of Canadian Bilateral Aid*, published in July 1976, by The Effectiveness Evaluation Division of the Planning Branch of the Treasury Board Secretariat. This document was kept classified until September 1983, when it was declassified in response to a request from Energy Probe.
2. *Partners in Development: Report of the Commission on International Development*, Praeger, 1969.
3. CBC's *The Fifth Estate*, April 4, 1978.
4. *Energy Probe's Statistical Handbook: The Other Energy Pie*, by David Poch, Energy Probe, Toronto, 1985. The national figures for energy use per capita and for energy use per unit of Gross Domestic Product given in Poch's book are based on data from the *U.N. Statistical Yearbook — 1981*, and the *OECD Main Economic Indicators*, Appendix.
5. One sorry example is an ill-fated semi-automatic bakery, built for Tanzania with Canadian aid in the early 1970s. The complex, which was supplied by a Canadian manufacturer of large-scale bakery equipment, began baking bread five years late and for twice the price that the same capacity bakery equipment could have been supplied by West German or Japanese manufacturers. And, in contrast to other bakeries in the capital city which employ high ceilings for air circulation, the Canadian-funded bakery, designed for the climatic conditions of Alberta, had a low ceiling with enclosed walls and a complex set of fans.

Because Tanzania is a net importer of wheat flour, Canadian aid is also funding the Basotu wheat growing scheme where "Canadian wheat farming practices as employed on the prairies may be introduced." See *Perpetuating Poverty: The Political Economy of Canadian Foreign Aid* by Robert Carty and Virginia Smith of the Latin America Working Group, Between the Lines, Toronto, 1981.

In order to transplant this energy-intensive agricultural system from Canada to Tanzania, traditional pastorists, the Barabegs, had to be displaced. According to Roger Young, author of *Canadian Development Assistance to Tanzania*, The North-South Institute, Ottawa, 1983, "Previously idle land is being brought under cultivation with the sophisticated technology of modern scientific research, mechanized agriculture and large-scale production."

6. According to Ontario Hydro's 1982 *Annual Report*, it "received about $9 million in revenue from these [international] activities." Among the CIDA contracts involving Ontario Hydro are the following:

- nine Ontario Hydro staff are training hydroelectric operators and maintenance employees for the Volta River Authority in Ghana (the body that oversees the Akosombo Dam, see chapter 2). The project also involves a data processing audit and the development of terms of reference for a management audit of the VRA,
- in 1971-73, Ontario Hydro provided a twelve man-year planning and engineering team to the Nigeria Niger Dams and helped bring the Kainji hydroelectric project into service,
- Ontario Hydro has supplied short-term assistance to CIDA projects in Botswana, Lesotho, Swaziland, and Egypt.

For more information see *Ontario Hydro Annual Reports* and *Foreign Projects Bimonthly and Quarterly Reports* available from Ontario Hydro, Toronto.

In 1978, Hydro-Québec assigned the task of exporting its know-how to a subsidiary, Hydro-Québec International. This subsidiary, which in 1982 alone earned $16 million, is currently concentrating its activities in Saudi Arabia, India, Bangladesh, Cameroon, Guinea Conakry, Argentina and Haiti. Among its international work is:

- a contract with the national electrical utility of Mali to provide coordination services for the country's first electricity and water supply project,
- a contract with Guinea Conakry to train a group of Guinean engineers at Hydro-Québec,
- marketing efforts in South America on transmission-line work and participation in studies for a nuclear power station,
- a $10 million technical cooperation agreement signed in the spring with the Société Nationale d'Electricité du Cameroun

(SONEL) which provides for a group of Hydro-Québec experts to be sent to SONEL and for future Cameroonian engineers to be trained in Québec.

See *Hydro-Québec Annual Reports* for the years 1982 and 1983 for more information.

7. In Ontario, for example, where power from small hydroelectric power plants was replaced with larger thermal electric generating plants, the small-scale hydro industry all but died out. Although it is undergoing a minor resurgence now, it faces an uphill battle because Ontario Hydro is not obligated to buy power from independent power producers who can generate power more cheaply than Ontario Hydro. The large-scale, centralized, monopoly approach to providing power prevails, and it is with this approach that Ontario Hydro and Hydro-Québec go into the Third World as advisors.

8. The Treasury Board found that $41.8 million in production would have been lost. Assuming a 15 percent profit on the $41.8 million, the lost benefit of that production amounts to only $6.27 million; assuming a 20 percent profit, the benefit lost is $8.36. By extrapolating from the Treasury Board's 1974 findings, we estimate that lost production for the 1982 year would have amounted to $75 million and the lost profit to between $11 million and $15 million. These compare unfavorably to the $135 million to $225 million taxpayers overpaid because the aid was tied.

9. The Treasury Board found that only $100 million difference in balance of payments would have resulted, or "only one-quarter of one percent of current account payments in 1974." This worsened balance of payments situation would not have hurt the economy at all, according to the Treasury Board report.

10. In the case of Canada's raw materials, price — not innovations — influences potential purchasers of wheat or timber, and in the case of manufactured goods where Canada lacks both the ability to innovate and the ability to compete, the argument is largely irrelevant "owing to the branch-plant nature of a large segment of our industry."

11. Holders of the Canadian dollars will eventually trade them in for Canadian goods and services (rather than continuing to exchange them for another country's goods or services or for another

country's currency). When they do, they are likely to purchase those goods and services for which Canadians are competitive producers. The unpredictability of this outcome for Canada's export picture is unnerving for a government that is trying to promote exports from particular industries, especially those in a slump. Seen in this light, tied aid is nothing more than a tool for promotion of particular exports. Critics such as Energy Probe and the North-South Institute ask only that a spade be called a spade. If the intention is to promote exports, the export promotion program should not be masquerading as a foreign aid program.

12. "Private sector must work to improve contract record," *Globe and Mail*, September 24, 1984.

13. "Ottawa's Aid/Trade Fund, a marriage of inconvenience" by Shelton Gordon, in *Globe and Mail*, April 20, 1984.

14. For an indication of who constitutes this business lobby and what their positions are, see the submission of the Canadian Manufacturing Association to the Parliamentary Task Force on North-South Relations, August 1980, and *Strengthening Canada Abroad*, the Final Report of the Export Promotion Review Committee (made up of representatives from 16 corporations) to the Minister of Industry, Trade and Commerce, November 30, 1979.

15. *Parliamentary Task Force on North-South Relations*, Report to House of Commons on the Relations Between Developed and Developing Countries, House of Commons, Canada, 1980.

16. *A Report on Canadians' Attitudes Toward Foreign Aid*, conducted and published by the Canadian International Development Agency, November 1980.

*Chapter 5*, pages 61-67

1. *Energy for Development* by John Foster, Efrain Friedmann, James W. Howe, Francisco R. Parra, and David H. Pollock, prepared for the North-South Roundtable of the Society for International Development, Praeger, 1981; and *Energy Strategies for Developing Countries* by J. Dunkerley, W. Ramsey, L. Gordon, E. Cecelski, Resources for the Future, John Hopkins University Press, 1981. Even when non-commercial fuels such as wood, cow dung, and other "traditional fuels," which are the main sources

of fuels for much of the Third World, are included, the industrial countries' energy consumption is still three times that of the Third World's.

2. *North-South: A Program for Survival*, the Report of the Independent Commission on International Development Issues, (also known as the Brandt Commission Report), 1980.

3. *Energy in the Developing Countries*, World Bank, August 1980.

4. This analysis was made by Anil Agarwal of the Centre for Science and Environment, New Delhi, in a paper presented to the December 1982 meeting of the NGO Taskforce on Alternative Approaches to Development in Geneva, entitled *Sustainable Development: Linkages Between North and South*.

5. *Tropical Moist Forests: The Resources, The People, The Threat* by Catherine Caufield, An Earthscan Paperback, London, 1982. See also, "Preservation and Production: Multinational Timber Corporations and Tropical Moist Forests" by Dr. Norman Myers, published in the Council on Economic Priorities *Newsletter*, CEP Publication N 0-5, September 1980.

6. See "Preservation and Production," *op. cit.*; and *Tropical Moist Forests*, *op. cit.*

7. *Tropical Moist Forests*, *op. cit.* Ironically, the Ivory Coast will lose not only its forests but also the foreign exchange earner it is plundering: one-quarter of its foreign exchange earnings come from forest product exports.

8. The causes of deforestation are still not well understood and, of course, vary from country to country. However it is becoming clear that, on a global scale, the collection of woodfuel is not the major cause of deforestation. Instead, the major cause of deforestation appears to be the clearing of land for farming, which includes cattle ranching, cash crop plantations, and subsistence agricultural by those who, for various reasons, are squeezed off their former lands. Logging, as pointed out in this chapter, is also a significant contributor, not only because it leaves a degraded forest in its wake but because the forest is soon cleared completely for agricultural purposes. Other causes include hydro dams, road building, and mining. In Brazil, for example, official figures attribute 38 percent of all deforestation in the Amazon between 1966 and 1975 to cattle ranching (most of which was encouraged with state financial

incentives); 31 percent to agriculture (over half state-sponsored); and 27 percent to highway construction. See *Tropical Moist Forests*, *op. cit.*, and *Tropical Forest Resources* by J.P. Lanly, FAO Forestry Paper No. 30, FAO, 1982.

9. For further information on the contribution of cattle ranching to deforestation, see "The Hamburger Connection: How Central America's Forests Become North America's Hamburgers" by Norman Myers, *Ambio*, Vol. 10, No. 1, 1981; *Tropical Forest Resources*, *op. cit.* and *Earth First*, Nevada, March 20, 1984.

10. "Rainforests and the Hamburger Society" by James D. Nations and Daniel I. Komer in *Environment*, Washington, April 1983.

11. "Moist Forest of the Tropics — A Plea for Protection and Development" by Robert O. Blake in *Journal '84*, World Resources Institute, Washington, 1984.

12. "Ecological wreckage is hidden cause of Salvador war," *Globe and Mail*, Sept 24, 1981, and *Ecodevelopment and International Cooperation* by Howard Daugherty, Charles Jeanneret-Grosjean and H.F. Fletcher, jointly published by Environment Canada and the Canadian International Development Agency in 1979.

*Chapter 6*, pages 68-75

1. "In defence of population growth" by Fred Pearce, *New Scientist*, August 9, 1984.

2. The World Bank in *World Development Report 1984*, its annual review of conditions in developing countries, predicted tragedy if population growth rates didn't come down. Another World Bank prediction, this time by its president, A. W. Clausen, appeared in "Too many mouths to feed," July 12, 1984, *Toronto Star*. Said Clausen: "For the poorest countries, development may not be possible at all unless slower population growth can be achieved soon." As described in "World population rise condemns millions to poverty," *Globe and Mail*, July 11, 1984: ".... population growth and economic development are inextricably linked. Without slowing population increases, developing nations will never achieve the economic and social development necessary to improve the lives of their citizenry, especially the poor."

3. "In defence of population growth," *op. cit.*
4. Haiti's annual rate of population increase, from the *U.N. Statistical Office Demographic Yearbook 1980*, was 1.8 percent while the Ivory Coast's was 3.5 percent. Both countries are faced with impending denuding of their landscapes. In Haiti, erosion is so pervasive that 14 million cubic yards of soil are washed into the sea each year. Rain when it does come, runs off so rapidly that flash floods make roads impassable and wash away the struggling crops. See *CUSO Forum*, Ottawa, Winter 1983. In the Ivory Coast, so few of the trees logged every year are replanted that the country's tropical forests could be eliminated this decade.
5. "In defence of population growth," *op. cit.*
6. *The Global 2000 Report to the President*, a report prepared by the Council on Environmental Quality and the Department of State, Washington, 1980.
7. The *Limits to Growth*, a Report for the Club of Rome's Project on the Predicament of Mankind by Donella H. Meadows, Dennis L. Meadows, Jorgen Randers, and Williams Behrens III, Universe Book, New York, 1972.
8. *Potential Population Supporting Capacities of Lands in the Developing World* by the Food and Agriculture Organization, 1983.
9. "Rural Energy Scarcity and Nutrition" by Srilatha Batliwala, *Economic and Political Weekly*, February 27, 1982.
10. Amulya Reddy describes in "Energy Options for the Third World" in *Southern Perspectives on the Rural Energy Crisis*, published by Nautilus, August 1981, how "In the absence of labor-saving devices and/or hired labor, these household energy needs become work schedules and time budgets for the members of the family, and these schedules and budgets can be achieved only when there are at least two or three children to help parents .... Such energy considerations are unfortunately completely ignored by population planners."

*Chapter 7*, pages 76-82

1. "The Tragedy of the Commons" by Garrett Hardin, published in *Science*, December 13, 1968.

2. For more information on fuelwood use see "Fuelwood and Charcoal in Developing Countries" by J. Arnold and J. Jongma in *Unasylva*, Vol. 29 No. 118, Food and Agriculture Organization, Rome, 1977; and *Fuelwood and Rural Energy: Production and Supply in the Humid Tropics* by R.R. Moss and W.B. Morgan, Tycooly International Publishing Ltd., Dublin, 1981.
3. "Forest Preservation in the Western Highlands of Guatemala" by Thomas T. Veblen, in *The Geographical Review*, October 1978.
4. *Social Economic and Ecological Impact of Social Forestry in Kolar* by V. Shiva, H.C. Sharatchandra, and J. Bandyopadhyay, published by Indian Institute of Management, Bangalore, India, 1981. The reason for the sustainable use of communal forests, explains the authors, was that the community was "a social organization based on commonly accepted norms and values which provide the organizing principles and control mechanisms for its members. A shared resource can be managed through community organization by the implicit acceptance on the part of all the members of a commonly shared norm for resource utilization."
5. *ibid.*
6. For more information on this contentious Bill see *The State of India's Environment: A Citizens' Report 1982* by the Centre for Science and Environment, New Delhi, 1982. Also see "The New Forest Bill: Old Wine in a Very Old Bottle" by V. Shiva, J. Bandyopadhyay, June 19, 1982, and "Forests for Industry's Profit" by K.P. Kannan, June 5, 1982, both in the *Economic and Political Weekly*, India.
7. *Deforestation in Kenya: A Case of Over-Exploitation of the Common-Property Resource?* by Patricia Adams, Master's Thesis, University of Sussex, England, August 1979.
8. *Tropical Moist Forests: The Resources, the People, The Threat* by Catherine Caufield, Earthscan Paperback, London, 1982.
9. All too often, this is not possible. Traditional coastal fishing villages in India provide an interesting example of why not. For centuries the exploitation of the common ocean resource was guided by rigid controls to which everyone — including the wealthier villagers — was subject. As a result, the marine resource was managed sustainably. Recently though, the rich villagers started using mechanized trawlers introduced through international and

local funding agencies. This has allowed them to take more than their share, causing a breakdown of community principles that had dictated equitable and sustainable fishing practices.

In addition to this influx of outside resources was the introduction of a market for fish. The commodities which these villages had once harvested for local use only were now exchanged for goods or money outside the village economy.

The richer villagers, who tended to have outside ties, were ideally placed to take advantage of the urban markets for fish that were opening up, and with these new markets they became independent of their village economies. This independence led to the erosion of the concepts of joint ownership and responsibility, an erosion reinforced by making ocean resources (such as fish) a "national" resource over which the state or federal governments had control. As long as individual villagers had been entirely dependent on their village economies to meet their needs they had a clear incentive to protect the resource base, which was the only basis of their sustenance.

Similarly, over-exploitation of the North American fishery began only when the North American Indians came into contact with the immigrant population and traders, who made fish a marketable commodity.

Says a Toronto economist, Peter Victor, "the cultural checks that historically had preserved the fishery were destroyed, giving rise to an example of what would currently be termed the 'tragedy of the commons'." He goes on to describe examples from history that indicate that the expansion of the market system created the tragedy of the commons by weakening the traditional forms of social relations which had once precluded over-exploitation of communal land.

For more on this interpretation see "Economics and the Challenge of Environmental Issues" by Peter A. Victor in *Ecology versus Politics in Canada*, edited by W. Leiss, University of Toronto Press, 1979; and *Social Economic and Ecological Impact of Social Forestry in Kolar*, *op. cit.*

10. "Forest Preservation in the Western Highlands of Guatemala," *op. cit.* Another example of a community which withstood outside pressures on their formerly well-managed environment is the Sher-

pa people of Nepal. B.A. Coburn, writing in *Nature and Resources*, July-September 1983, in an article entitled, "Managing Himalayan World Heritage Site," describes the effect of China's takeover of Tibet in 1959.
'Waves of refugees fled Tibet, crossing the Nangpa La and other high passes with their livestock, passing through — some settling in — Khumba [Nepal]. In Tibet, trees were scarce; the unaccustomed abundance of Khumbu's forests prompted a lavish use of local forest resources that scandalized resident Sherpas, who found their regulatory institutions largely disregarded. One resident of Namche asserted that the Tibetans burned two loads of wood (approximately 60 kilograms) per day, compared to the Sherpas' conservation half load .... before the migration from Tibet there was more than enough grass for all the cattle, but the extensive bands of sheep and other livestock brought from the far side of the Himalayas 'ate the grass to the ground' .... starvation and disease eventually decimated those animals, along with the Sherpas' herds, though they have recovered enough to sustain some numbers at the carrying capacity of the pasturage. The pastures and forests have not fully recovered."

*Chapter 8*, pages 83-90

1. "Progress palls Katmandu's idyllic setting," *Globe and Mail*, December 19, 1983.
2. The link was important to the viability of Ontario Hydro's nuclear expansion program. Because the growth in electrical demand in Ontario had fallen, the importance of export markets to reduce Hydro's surplus generating capacity was increasing. Initially, the cable would primarily carry coal-fired electricity, but as Hydro's new reactors came on line, nuclear electricity would have phased out coal-fired electricity.
3. For more information on the G.P.U. electricity export deal see *The Employment Cost of Electricity Exports: The GPU Sale* and *The GPU Deal: A Cost-Benefit Analysis of Ontario Hydro's Proposed Sale of Coal-Fired Electricity to General Public Utilities*, both written by Jack O. Gibbons and published by Energy Probe in 1982.

4. *Energy Shock* by Lawrence Solomon, Doubleday, Toronto, 1980.
5. *The State of India's Environment 1982: A Citizens' Report* by the Centre for Science and Environment, New Delhi, India, 1982.
6. India's Lost Woodlands" by Modhumita Mojumdar in *The Christian Science Monitor*, September 8, 1981.
7. *ibid.*
8. *Problems of the Management of Bamboo Resources in Tamil Nadu* by S. Ramesh Bhatt, published by The Bombay Natural History Society, India, 1982.
9. *ibid.*
10. *The State of India's Environment*, *op. cit.*
11. "Brazil, Energy and the Amazon" by Catherine Caufield in *New Scientist*, October 28, 1982. For more information on the environmental problems associated with hydro dams in tropical forests see "Defoliant Clouds a Rainforest's Future" by Catherine Caufield, *New Scientist*, August 26, 1982.
12. "Brazil, Energy and the Amazon," *op. cit.*
13. *ibid.*
14. *Human Impact on the Aquatic Ecosystem of the Rio Lempa, El Salvador* by Monica Elizabeth Ewert, M.E.S. Thesis, Faculty of Environmental Studies, York University, Toronto, 1978.
15. "Brazil, Energy and the Amazon," *op. cit.*
16. *ibid.*
17. The problem of the paucity of trees was recognized by the Sri Lankan government and by the Western aid-giving governments early on. But it wasn't until 1981 that a replanting program began with a goal to replant 30% of the hillside, or over 400,000 acres. By the end of 1982 however, only about 1,000 acres had been replanted, primarily because the cost of the Mahaweli Program has more than doubled. The Sri Lankan government, in its attempt to find funds, has cut monies allocated to preparation of new agricultural land for the new settlers and for reforestation. For more information on this project see "Big Dam Schemes — Value for Money or Non-sustainable Development?" by John Madeley in *Mazingira*, Vol.7. No.4. 1983; *The Truth about the Mahaweli* by Gamini Iriyagolle, O.U.P.; "Mahaweli Development Project: An Economic Disaster?" by Ahmed Hugue in *Lanka Guardian*,

Sri Lanka, July 1, 1982; "Dam costly place to be poor" by John Madeley in *The Guardian*, London, May 5, 1984; "Leaks and landslide loom in Sri Lanka" by John Madeley, *New Scientist*, London, April 7, 1983; and "Sri Lanka's energy problem comes out of the woods," *New Scientist*, August 13, 1981.
18. "Dam costly place to be poor," *op. cit.*

*Chapter 9*, pages 91-95

1. "Ganges Plain cited as big threat to ecology" in *Globe and Mail*, Toronto, May 16, 1984.
2. In 1983, scientific evidence showed, more precisely than ever before, the movement of water in the Amazon rainforest. See "Recycling of water by forest is found to affect weather," in *Globe and Mail*, Toronto, July 15, 1983.
3. For the information and examples given in this chapter we are indebted to the excellent report of The Centre for Science and Environment, *The State of India's Environment 1982 — A Citizens' Report*, New Delhi. The product of some 40 citizens groups, this book is a wealth of examples and analyses of India's major environmental problems.
4. *ibid.*
5. *ibid.*
6. "Ganges Plain cited as big threat to ecology," *op. cit.*
It was floods like these that provided the genesis of the Chipko movement in the Himalayas. As described in *Hugging the Himalaya: The Chipko Experience*, edited by Shishupal Singh Kunwar and published by Dasholi Gram Swarajya Mandal, Gopeshwar (Champoli) U.P. India, March 1982:

> The Alakananda Valley in which the movement originated was the scene of an unprecedented flood in 1970. The entire village of Belakuchi was washed away by the swirling torrent of the Alakananda .... The flood affected an area spread over a length of 400 km and washed away five major bridges, hundreds of head of cattle and several million rupees' worth of timber and fuel. The silt carried by the flood waters was so enormous that a 10 km stretch of the Upper Ganga Canal, which is some 350 km from the upper reaches of the Alakan-

anda, became blocked. Subsequent desilting operations took so much time that western UP's farm output nose dived that year through lack of irrigation water.

This Alakananda tragedy left a deep impression on the hill-folk and, with it, soon followed the appreciation of the role that forests play in their lives. They had also watched the slow replacement of broad-leaf forests by economically important species like the pine and had slowly felt the deleterious effects of this policy on their cultivation and water supply. While oak leaves, for instance, give rise to a nutrient-rich water-absorbing humus, pine needles do not decompose and allow the precipitation to run off. An oak forest, therefore, holds on to water for a long time and releases it very slowly. This gives rise to perennial streams and rivulets, around which hill village communities have come to be established over the ages. But the oak, unfortunately, does not happen to be an economically important tree. As a result, it has been indiscriminately felled without any concern for the ecological imbalances this would create.

An interesting billboard in Gopeshwar, set up by the Chipko leaders, declares: "One oak tree draws from the atmosphere 400 gallons of water each day. Cut one oak tree and the rivers and streams will lose 400 gallons of water. Forests are not merely for beauty; our entire food systems are dependent on them. If it ever becomes necessary to cut a tree, remember if one tree is cut three new saplings will have to be planted to make up the damage. Avoid cutting one tree, or else plant three new trees."

Indeed, it was this recognition of the forests as their lifeblood that motivated the women of the Himalayas to protect the trees from the loggers' axe by hugging the trees. It was this action that gave rise to the movement's name — Chipko Andolan, which literally means "movement to embrace."

7. Also see *Planting for the Future: Forestry for Human Needs* by Erik Eckholm, Worldwatch Paper No. 26, February 1979. and "Forest Destruction in Asia and the South Pacific," by M.K Ranjitsinh in *Ambio*, Vol. 8. No 5, 1979.

8. "China's Floods and Forests," by Wang Yun (China Features

newsagency, China) duplicated in *Earthscan Bulletin*, February 1982.

9. The Sri Lankan Ministry for Plan Implementation said in a 1981 document that "if there is no proper vegetation cover, the rain water would on impact cause soil erosion and flow down the hill slopes in gushes, eroding the soil cover in its path. The fast water would bring down silt to the riverbed." From "Big Dam Schemes — Value for Money or Non-sustainable Development?" by John Madeley, in *Mazingira*, Vol. 7, No. 4, 1983.

*Chapter 10*, pages 96-107

1. "Stop the Dams? Tucurui and the Hope for Change," comments by Dr. Robert Goodland at a workshop on *Hydroelectric Projects and Native Peoples* sponsored by the Anthropology Resource Center. Published in *The Global Reporter*, a publication of ARC, Summer 1983.

2. Including the U.N. Development Program, the U.N. Environment Program, the World Bank, the Asian, African, Caribbean and Inter-American Development Banks, the Arab Bank for Economic Development in Africa, The Organization of American States, and the Commission of the European Communities, who together lent over $18 billion to fund projects in Third World countries in 1982.

3. *The Volta River Project: A Case Study in Politics and Technology* by David Hart, University Press, Edinburgh, 1980.

4. "Indigenous People 'Developed' Out of Their Lands," by Steve Billes in *Multinational Monitor*, September 1983. See also *The World Bank: A Critical Analysis* by Cheryl Payer, Monthly Review Press, New York 1982.

5. The project, known as the Polonoroeste Project, threatens to wipe out nearly all of Brazil's remaining Indian tribes. The scheme will open up Brazil's north-western provinces of Mato Grosso and Rondonia — an area of jungle and savanna bigger than Great Britain. This will mean roads, farms, ranches, and settlers which, for the Indian tribes, will bring not progress but all the ills of the modern world. These ills include diseases such as measles and the common cold, against which the Indians have no immunity.

Through the wholesale destruction of forests — the habitat which is the basis of the Indians' livelihood and culture — the Indians will soon be extinct. Price's study stated that FUNAI, the official Brazilian body which is supposed to protect Indian rights, was not to be trusted to implement guarantees to reserve land for the tribespeople. For example, FUNAI's head, Colonel Joao Carlos Nobre de Veiga, said the Indians had quite enough land already. See *Survival International Review*, Vol. 6, No. 3, and No. 4, Autumn 1981, and "Indians go on warpath against World Bank" by Rosemary Righter in *The Sunday Times*, London, March 1, 1981.

6. *The World Bank: A Critical Analysis*, *op. cit.*

7. Despite the claims of aid officials in many countries that it is nearly impossible to attach conditions to foreign aid loans if they affect the domestic political situation of recipient countries, conditions are not without precedent. Before funding a project in Peru that would settle 150,000 families in three river valleys inhabited by Amuesha Indians, America's AID sought guarantees that the Amuesha would receive "legal title to, or legal permits for the use and employment of, their tribal lands." AID also required certain guarantees against environmental degradation. For more information on this see Survival International *Information Packages* on the Pichis-Palcazu Development Project in Peru, and *The Global Reporter*, Anthropology Resource Center, Washington, Spring 1984.

8. *Environmental Guidelines Survey: An Analysis of Environmental Procedures and Guidelines Governing Development Aid* by John Horberry, for the Joint Environmental Service of the International Union for Conservation of Nature and Natural Resources and the International Institute for Environment and Development, 1983. This study was commissioned for the Committee of International Development Institutions on the Environment.

9. *Statement to the Subcommittee on International Development Institutions and Finance of the Committee on Banking, Finance and Urban Affairs*, by John Horberry, June 28, 1983 at the U.S. Congressional Hearings on the Environmental Impact of Multilateral Development Bank-Funded Projects.

10. *The Inter-American Development Bank and the*

*Environment*, Inter-American Development Bank, May 1983. This position was reiterated in a letter from the IDB Manager of the Project Analysis Department to Energy Probe, September 14, 1984.

Unfortunately, this evaluation of environmental factors, which the Bank considers "essential of every stage of the project cycle," is conducted in secret. The letter's author, Luis Fernando Jaramillo, claimed that the IDB's "internal working relationships, both formal and informal, create a most effective atmosphere for sharing of knowledge and risk perceptions which are so important in the search for integrated multidisciplinary solutions to complex environmental issues." But people who must live with the consequences of a project, anywhere in the world, are rarely content to allow the evaluation of risk to be made by a few outsiders behind closed doors.

11. "The Challenge of Sustainable Development" by Bruce M. Rich in *The Global Reporter*, Anthropology Resource Center, Fall 1983. This article was also excerpted from Bruce Rich's statement to the U.S. Congressional Hearings of the Subcommittee on the International Development Institutions and Finance of the Committee on Banking, Finance and Urban Affairs, June 1983.

12. "Stop the Dams? Tucurui and the Hope for Change," *op. cit.*

13. "The Challenge of Sustainable Development," *op. cit.*

14. *The Environment and Bilateral Development Aid* by Brian Johnson and Robert O. Blake for the International Institute for Environment and Development. Washington and London. 1980.

15. The Mackenzie Valley pipeline hearings conducted under the direction of the Honourable Thomas Berger have become a model for indigenous rights groups, as well as for environmentalists and economic planners who advocate caution when it comes to implementing enormous projects with such dramatic implications for the environment and the indigenous peoples of the north. The Commission recommended that the gas pipeline be postponed for ten years in order for the Dene and the Canadian governments to negotiate aboriginal land rights. The other Commission, into Ontario Hydro's electric power plans, provided a much needed public review of the province's nuclear power expansion program.

16. The leverage of aid, *Globe and Mail*, Aug 20, 1984; "Leaks

and landslide loom in Sri Lanka," *New Scientist*, April 7, 1983; and "Canadian assistance aids suppressions in Sri Lanka," *Calgary Herald*, February 4, 1983.

17. Letter from Guido A. Lucha, IDB Representative, June 24, 1982 (IDB Reference No. 604/82-FHA) to Father Pierre Salvetti, Parish of Verrettes, Haiti.

18. *Haiti un Choix de Dêveloppement: Barrages Hydro-Electriques ou Production Agricole?* by Comité Francais de Défense des Droits de l'Homme en Haiti, Lyon, France, 1981.

19. A comment from an IDB official who asked to remain anonymous.

20. See correspondence between Energy Probe and William McWhinney, Acting President of CIDA, from March 21, 1983 to November 28, 1983. The head of Public Affairs of the IDB, Mr. M. Czarnecki, also refused to comment on the study in a telephone conversation in March 1983.

21. "Missionaries Rap Dam Projects" by Diane Jensen, *Ottawa Citizen*, October 16, 1982.

22. "The Unbelievable Quarrels between the IMF and a Corrupt Regime," in *Le Monde Diplomatique*, France, May 20, 1983.

23. From the correspondence between the Canadian Secretary of State for External Affairs, Allan MacEachen, and Canadian citizens who wrote to the minister regarding the issue of aid to hydrodams in the Third World. This quote was from a January 23, 1984 letter from MacEachen.

24. "Dam the Chico: Hydropower Development and Tribal Resistance" by Charlie Drucker, 1984, for publication by *The Ecologist*, U.K.

25. *ibid.* After violence in the Chico Valley broke out the World Bank withdrew funding for the dams. They have, however, remained the principal funder for the Chico River Irrigation Project which is dependent on the building of one of the Chico dams (Chico IV). Survival International also reports in its *Information Pack: Update Chico Dam Projects: Philippines* IP/PHI/16/April 1983, that World Bank funds are being transferred to other dam projects affecting the Ifugao and other Filipino tribal peoples.

26. See notes 1 and 2 in the Preface.

27. See note 23 in this chapter and note 2 in the Preface.

28. Hearings before the Subcommittee of International Development Institutions and Finance of the Committee on Banking Finance and Urban Affairs, House of Representatives Ninety-Eighth Congress, June 1983. Because of these hearings another congressional committee — the House Science and Technology Committee, Subcommittee on National Resources, Agriculture Research and the Environment — held a hearing on the environmental side-effects of Third World aid projects in September 1984, and is expected to hold more hearings in the next congressional session.
29. *North-South: A Program for Survival.* The report of the Independent Commission on International Development Issues under the Chairmanship of Willy Brandt, the MIT Press, Cambridge, Massachusetts, 1980.
30. "The Secrecy at Work in Poverty Politics" by Helen Pace in *The Guardian*, January 14, 1981.

*Chapter 11*, pages 111-115

1. Based on 1982 figures from Energy Mines and Resources' *Electric Power in Canada: 1982*, and Statscan's *Electric Power Statistics*, Vol. 1, for Canada; and on *Electrical World*, December 1982 for the U.S. Some surplus, of course, is prudent for unexpected contingencies. According to *A New Prosperity*, a report commissioned by the U.S. Department of Energy, Brick House Publishing, 1981, a surplus of 15% to 20% is "an amount most analysts would agree can provide adequate reliability for a typical utility system." North America's surplus is, in other words, two to three times what is required.
2. "U.S. nuclear power costing more than coal plants" from the New York Times Service, in the *Globe and Mail*, September 8, 1984.
3. As an indication of how wildly optimistic energy planners became, the Canadian federal department of Energy, Mines and Resources' major policy statement, *An Energy Policy for Canada-Phase I* (1973), planned on Canada building the equivalent of one 500-megawatt reactor every 1.4 days, or about 2,600 per decade, by the year 2040. Current plans have wiped out almost all of these Canadian reactors, as have current plans in the U.S., which have

scaled down U.S. needs by tens of thousands of reactors. Also see *Night Descends on the Nuclear Dream: Economics of Coal, Nuclear Energy and Conservation in the United States, France, Germany, United Kingdom and the Soviet Union*, by Jim Harding, published by the International Project for Soft Energy Paths, San Francisco, 1984.

4. Amory and Hunter Lovins explain in "Good News About Energy," *New Age*, October 1980, that in the U.S.A. in the same period, 72 percent of new energy "found" came from conservation: "we already got from efficiency improvements twice as much energy 'supplying' capacity twice as fast as the synthetic fuels people say they can do at ten times the cost." Historically, gross national product was thought to increase (or decrease) in lockstep with available energy supplies such as oil, gas, coal, solar energy or uranium. Then after the oil crisis of the 1970s, energy economists began to realize that it wasn't energy in its primary form that was critical to economic growth but the energy services — such as heating, cooking, lighting and mechanical motion — provided by these energy supplies. If they could squeeze more usefulness — more of these energy services — out of existing supplies, then GNP would increase. And increase it did, not with more energy in its primary form but with less, because we were using less energy more efficiently and fueling economic growth with conservation.

5. *Kenya: Issues and Options in the Energy Sector*, Report of the Joint UNDP/World Bank Energy Sector Assessment Program, Report No. 3800-KE, May 1982.

6. *Energy for Development: An International Challenge* by John Foster, Efrain Friedmann, James W. Howe, Francisco R. Parra, and David Pollock, Praeger Publishers, New York, 1981.

*Chapter 12*, pages 116-121

1. Transcript of Panel on the Role of Nuclear Power, Symposium II, 1982 World's Fair International Energy Symposia, Knoxville, Tennessee, November 3, 1981. Transcript available from the Canadian Coalition for Nuclear Responsibility, Montreal.

2. "The next nuclear power?" in *The Economist*, September 15, 1979.

3. *ibid.*
4. For an excellent reference to nuclear power in the Third World see *The Nuclear Fix: A Guide to Nuclear Activities in the Third World* by Thijs de la Court, Deborah Pick and, Daniel Nordquist of the World Information Service on Energy, The Netherlands, 1982.
5. "Slowdown of Brazil's energy program is a setback for suppliers of equipment," *Globe and Mail*, Report on Business, March 29, 1982, Toronto. See also "Brazil struggles with nuclear power," *New Scientist*, May 17, 1984.
6. "Mexico may defer nuclear plan" in *Globe and Mail*, April 7, 1982. "Nuclear industry is stalled despite economic gains," *Globe and Mail*, Report on Business, Toronto, January 16, 1984. In fact, developing countries are not alone in being threatened with unmanageable nuclear power-induced foreign debts. After Mexico and Brazil comes France with the world's third largest foreign debt of $50 billion, of which over $10 billion is the result of Electricité de France's nuclear program. See also *Night Descends on the Nuclear Dream: Economics of Coal, Nuclear Energy and Conservation in the United States, France, Germany, United Kingdom and Soviet Union* by Jim Harding, International Project for Soft Energy Paths, San Francisco, 1984.
7. "Power to the people: high-wire act of a plug-in society," *The Christian Science Monitor*, June 10, 1983.
8. "Why Canada Should Stop Selling Its Reactors to Third World Nations" by D.W.O. Rogers in *Science Forum*, October 1977.
9. *Nuclear Power: The Market Test* by Christopher Flavin, published by Worldwatch Institute in Washington, D.C., 1983; and *Night Descends on the Nuclear Dream* by Jim Harding, *op. cit.* Harding estimates in his study that in the U.S. costs over ten years are expected to average about 12 cents/kwh for nuclear reactors, 6.2 cents/kwh for coal plants, and 6.5 cents/kwh for the very modest amount of oil capacity.
10. For more information on this subject see "Pushing Reactors" by Joseph R. Egan in *New York Times*, January 26, 1982; "Mini-reactors could mean nuclear boom for small nations," by David T. Shapiro; and *The interdependent* published by the U.N. Association, U.S.A. 1982. See also "AECL studies small reactors for

Third World market," *Globe and Mail*, Report on Business, June 1, 1984.
11. *The Energy Transition in Developing Countries*, The World Bank, 1983.
12. This figure, of course, varies from one country to another. In Tanzania about 55 percent of oil used domestically is used in the transportation sector. In Nepal the comparable figure is 60 percent and for Kenya it is 55 percent.

*Chapter 13*, pages 122-128

1. *The Myth of TVA, Conservation and Development in the Tennessee Valley, 1933 — 1983* by William U. Chandler with Environmental Policy Institute, Ballinger Publishing Company, Washington, 1984.
2. In addition to William Chandler's book, *The Myth of TVA* (note 1), see also *Cities and the Wealth of Nations* by Jane Jacobs, Random House, New York, 1984, in which she describes the TVA region as an "artificial city region" which has never developed the capacity to produce "amply and diversely for its own producers and people as well as others." It has thus ".... continued to depend on importing almost everything or else going without."

It is fascinating to note that the TVA became the model for subsequent massive river development schemes in the Third World, including the Volta River Authority in Ghana, and that the TVA has worked under contract to AID, providing assistance on energy projects in the Philippines, Indonesia, Egypt, and many Latin American countries.
3. This assessment, originally by Bruce Netschert, appears in *The Myth of TVA*, *op. cit.*
4. *Annual Report* of the Philippines National Electrification Administration, 1979.
5. *The Socio-Economic Impact of Rural Electrification in Developing Countries: A Review of Evidence* by Fred Fluitman, World Employment Program Research Working Paper 126 from the International Labor Organization, Geneva, November 1983.
6. The fact that only one-tenth of the total investment in the electric

power sector has gone to rural electrification comes as a surprise considering the attention it has received as the panacea for rural development. But when compared to the meager amount that has gone to the development of renewable forms of energy such as biomass, which presently meet the majority of the rural populations energy needs, this investment seems disproportionately high. See *Rural Electrification: A World Bank Paper*, The World Bank, Washington, October 6, 1975.

7. That more recent data on the extent of rural electrification is not available underscores the point that vast sums of money are spent to provide a service, the need for which is largely unknown. See *Rural Electrification: A World Bank Paper, op. cit.*

8. *Energy for Development: Third World Options* by Denis Hayes, Worldwatch Paper 15, December 1977.

9. "Dazzling Darkness," editorial in *Economic and Political Weekly*, Bombay, December 15, 1979. The cost of electrifying a rural Indian home (500 to 800 rupees) would be between $80 to $125 dollars.

10. *Rural Electrification: A World Bank Paper, op. cit.*

11. "Rural Electrification: Towards a Crisis in Confidence" in *Soft Energy Notes*, May, 1979.

12. *ibid.*

13. *The Socio-Economic Impact of Rural Electrification in Developing Countries, op. cit.*

14. *Bolivia: Rural Electrification*, AID Project Impact Evaluation Report No. 16, December 1980.

15. This quote is found in the *The Socio-Economic Impact of* Rural Electrification in Developing Countries, op. cit., *but comes from an internal report of the Inter-American Development Bank, entitled* Evaluation report on rural electrification and energy, *Washington, D.C., June 1979.*

16. *The Product Is Progress: Rural Electrification in Costa Rica*, AID Project Impact Evaluation Report No. 22, October 1981.

17. The quote, which appears in *The Socio-Economic Impact of Rural Electrification in Developing Countries, op. cit.*, was originally from *Cooperative rural electrification: case studies of pilot projects in Latin America* by J.E. Ross, Praeger, New York, 1972.

18. The quote appears in *The Socio-Economic Impact of Rural Electrification in Developing Countries, op. cit.*, but comes originally from "Rural Electrification in Pakistan," in R.A. Stanford's *Rural Development in Pakistan*, Carolina Academic Press, Durham N. C., 1980.
19. The ILO study concludes that declining birth rates in the Third World are the result of a whole myriad of social and economic changes, only one of which is the introduction of electricity. Even this, they considered of marginal importance.
20. Correspondence from James J. Fish, World Bank, to Energy Probe, February 15, 1984. The target for 1982 to 1992, however, is unlikely to be met, he says, "given the current state of the world economy .... rural electrification programs are frequently the first casualties when resources are constrained."
21. *The Socio-Economic Impact of Rural Electrification in Developing Countries: A Review of Evidence, op. cit.*

*Chapter 14*, pages 129-134

1. "The U.N. Water Decade — PV pumpers key to billion-dollar market" in *Renewable Energy News*, March 1984. "PV" is a solar industry trade term for a photovoltaic cell, a device that converts light into electrical energy. The cell is a small wafer made of treated silicon or other semiconductor material.
2. "Foreign Markets Are Main Outlet For Canadian Solar E xpertise," *Globe and Mail*, Report on Business, October 5, 1981.
3. "Keeping Energy Costs Down No Help to Solar Industry," *Globe and Mail*, Report on Business, October 5, 1981.
4. Notes for Remarks by the Prime Minister of Canada at the U.N. Conference on New and Renewable Sources of Energy, Nairobi, August 11, 1981.

Of the $40 million pledged, $10 million was for Canada's International Development Research Centre to support energy research in Third World countries, $5 million was for private companies in Canada to encourage exports of new energy technologies to the Third World, and $25 million was for the Canadian International Development Agency to provide the African Sahel region with Canadian goods and services in energy and reforestation.

5. "How We're Selling Solar Tech Abroad," *Toronto Star*, August 31, 1981.

6. *Working Paper on Research and Technological Capacity for the Use of Renewable Energy Resources in Developing Countries*, by C. Weiss (et al), World Bank Working Paper prepared by Science and Technology Unit, Projects Advisory Services, World Bank, 1980.

7. The survey was assembled by J. Howe and D. Gallick for their report, *Fuelwood and Renewable Energy Projects in Africa: A Review of Donor Agency Programmes*, Overseas Development Council, Washington D.C., 1980 and is described in *Renewable Energy Technologies and the Third World: Issues in Transfer and Development of Technology* (see note 8). It is based on an International Energy Agency inventory, data from the Solar Energy Research Institute in Colorado, and on a report entitled *Energy in Developing Countries Subject Report: Development Assistance in the Field of Energy*, prepared for the Swedish International Development Agency in 1979.

The agencies in these surveys include, among the multilaterals, the European Economic Community, the Economic Commission for Africa, the Food and Agriculture Organization, the U.N. Educational, Scientific and Cultural Organization, the U.N. Industrial Development Organization, the U.N. Development Program, the U.N. University, the World Food Program, The U.N. Center for Human Settlements, and the U.N. Committee on Natural Resources, Energy and Transportation. Among the bilateral agencies, those of West Germany, France, Canada, U.S.A., Belgium, Ireland, Kuwait, Switzerland, the Netherlands, Austria, Italy, Sweden, the U.K., Japan, Denmark and Norway were included. The 175 renewable energy technology projects referred to excludes hydroelectric and forestry projects.

8. *Renewable Energy Technologies and the Third World: Issues in the Transfer and Development of Technology*, a Science Policy Research Unit (SPRU — at the University of Sussex) mimeo prepared by Kurt Hoffman for UNCTAD Secretariat, Technology Division, Geneva, July 1981.

9. *Renewable Energy Technologies and the Third World: Issues in the Transfer and Development of Technology, op. cit.* Data of a qualitative nature only was kept. For further information see *Solar Technologies: State of the Art Studies and Some of the Issues Impeding their Growth in Developing Countries*, mimeo by M.A.S. Malik published by the Solar Energy Research Institute, Colorado, in February 1980.
10. "Is Third World a Solar Guinea Pig?" *Globe and Mail*, August 18, 1979.
11. "Technology — to Buy or Not?" by Gamini Seneviratne in *Renews 6*, the NGO Newspaper for the U.N. Conference on New and Renewable Sources of Energy, Nairobi, Kenya, August 1981.
12. "PV pump development gets $15 million CIDA boost" in *Renewable Energy News*, March 1984.

Hoffman describes the basis of the Third World's fear that they are being used as guinea pigs in his SPRU mimeo, *Renewable Energy Technologies and the Third World, op. cit.* The quick penetration of "near term" Third World markets is "considered to be an essential stage in the expansion of the domestic industry, allowing it to accumulate experience, build up capacity and reduce prices to a level adequate to open up the longer term but much more sizeable markets in the advanced industrial economies. This strategy is enshrined in virtually every policy statement emanating from the public sector in the developed countries and from the EEC."
13. "Exxon unloading PV business disaster" in *Renewable Energy News*, November 1983.
14. "Technology — to Buy or Not?" *op. cit.*

*Chapter 15*, pages 135-138

1. "Renewable bio-solar and microbial systems in 'eco-rural' development," *Impact of Science on Society*, Volume 30, No. 3, 1980. This is compared to 20.4 percent of Canada's secondary energy consumption that comes from renewable energy, the bulk of which, 14.2 percent, is hydroelectric power. See *Energy Probe's Statistical Handbook: The Other Energy Pie*, by David Poch, Energy Probe, Toronto 1985.

2. *ibid.*
3. *Forest Energy and Economic Development*, by David Earl, Clarendon Press, Oxford, 1975.
4. *From a Pyramid to a Sphere*, paper presented to the "Global Connections" Seminar on Energy Development, Toronto, by Janos Pasztor, from the World Council of Churches, May 7, 1982. Available from Energy Probe, Toronto.

Also, according to the World Bank, "if fuelwood and agricultural and animal residues are included in the national energy balance, the household sector is the largest energy user in most developing countries, accounting for almost half of the total energy used in most of these countries and up to 90 percent in some of them (for example, Burundi, Malawi, Nepal and Rwanda)," *The Energy Transition in Developing Countries*, The World Bank, 1983.
5. "Energy Options for the Third World" by Amulya Reddy in *Southern Perspectives on the Rural Energy Crisis*, edited and published by Nautilus, California, August 1981.
6. "Animal Power Muscles Ahead" by Noel D. Vietmeyer in *International Wildlife*, September-October 1982. This article notes that India's bullocks and water buffaloes haul more freight each year than its railroads. In 1981, Prime Minister Indira Gandhi reported at the U.N. Conference on New and Renewable Sources of Energy that animals in India represented a potential power source of 30,000 megawatts — 1,000 megawatts more than the country's electrical power plants. Overall in the developing world, there are about 100 working animals for every working tractor, and in Southeast Asia more than 90 percent of the total available agricultural power comes from the muscles of cattle and water buffaloes.
7. "Energy options for the Third World," *op. cit.* Human labor accounts for 27 percent, bullock power for 62 percent, oil for 3.7 percent and electricity for 6.9 percent of all the energy used in the agricultural activities of the typical Indian village Dr. Reddy studied.

*Chapter 16*, pages 139-146

1. Traditional stoves in the Third World come in all shapes and

sizes and are made from a wide variety of materials including stones, clay, and metal. The most common method of cooking, especially in rural areas, is over an open fire occasionally circled by three or more stones, bricks, mounds of mud or lumps of other incombustible material. The stones act as supports for the cooking pot which is positioned over the center of the fire. In the urban areas, enclosed metal or ceramic stoves made by local ironsmiths or potters are more common.

The fuels used in these hundreds of different kinds of stoves have one thing in common — they are biomass in one form or another. For example, three-stone stoves usually use wood, metal stoves usually use charcoal, and anything from crop residue and animal dung to wood and charcoal (and combinations of these) may be burnt in traditional stoves found throughout the world.

*VITA News*, Virginia, U.S.A., January 1984, reports that researchers are discovering that they jumped too quickly to conclusions about the efficiency of traditional cooking methods. New tests measuring the efficiency of rural, three-stone stoves in real-life conditions show that, when skillfully tended by a Third World woman, their efficiency can be double what was found in the laboratory. Contrary to the numerous claims that the traditional three-stone stove captures only five percent of the heat value of the wood, research by Upper Volta's Voltaic Institute of Energy found three-stone stoves to have actual efficiencies ranging from ten to twenty-two percent with an average of about seventeen percent.

For more information on different cooking techniques, the function of traditional stoves around the world, and difficulties encountered by attempts to introduce more efficient wood stoves, see *Improved Cooking Stove in Developing Countries* by Gerald Foley and Patricia Moss, Earthscan Energy Information Programme, 1983; *The Woodfuel Problem and the Diffusion of Rural Innovations* by Bina Agarwal for the U.K. Tropical Products Institute, 1980, London; and *Boiling Point*, a newsletter of the Intermediate Technology Development Group Stoves Project, Reading, U.K.

2. Solar cooker designs vary. One Toronto scientist invented an ingenious solar cooker in a suitcase. When opened the inside of the top, which is lined with aluminium foil, acts as a reflector for sunlight directed onto a blackened cookie pan, which then radiates

through the pan and heats a chamber that has been insulated to hold in heat. Other designs were less ingenious. One parabolic reflector focussed the sun's rays on a pot of food but, unfortunately, burned the cook whose hand would inevitably cross the path of the sun's focussed rays.

3. The requirements of these stoves are as varied as the number of communities throughout the Third World. In India, women in one Himalayan village wanted, above all else, to reduce the smoke exhaust from their stoves. The smoke was not needed to keep mosquitoes away from their roofs because the roofs were made of tile and dung. In Upper Volta, the Voltaic Institute of Energy found a need for new and improved stoves that could provide space heating in the winter or in cold climates, yet could be adjusted to produce less heat in the kitchen during the warm season. They also discovered a market for a stove that could evacuate most smoke from a kitchen, but leave enough inside to repel termites and mosquitoes, preserve food in the rafters, and to waterproof the thatch. In Botswana, where the traditional hearth serves as a social center, villagers prefer a stove with a front which can be opened to provide heat and light.

4. "Fire Without Smoke" by Rajiv Gupta, Centre for Science and Environment Information Service, New Delhi, India, 1982.

5. *ibid.*

*Chapter 17*, pages 151-166

1. From correspondence between the Canadian Taskforce on the Churches and Corporate Responsibility and Marc Lalonde, the Canadian Minister of Finance, March 8, 1984.

2. For example, of the $4.866 billion in loans that Canada's Export Development Corporation facilitated during 1983, at least half went to Third World countries. For more information see Export Development Corporation *Annual Report — 1983* and *Statistical Review — 1983*, Ottawa. In many cases the distinction between the aid program and the trade promotion program is blurred by the joint funding of projects. It was blurred even further in February 1984 when the Canadian Minister of Finance announced in his budget speech that half of the aid budget's increase, worth up

to $1.3 billion by 1990, would go into an aid-trade fund to be used to finance projects in tandem with the credit facilities of the Export Development Corporation. See *The Budget Speech*, delivered in the House of Commons by the Honourable Marc Lalonde, Minister of Finance, February 15, 1984.

3. "Blaming the West for Third World Poverty," a review by Paul Craig Roberts in *The Wall Street Journal*, August 27, 1984 of *Reality and Rhetoric: Studies in the Economics of Development* by Peter Bauer, Book Centre, 1984.

4. *ibid.*

5. *The World Bank: A Critical Analysis*, by Cheryl Payer, Monthly Review Press, New York, 1982.

6. *Cities and the Wealth of Nations*, by Jane Jacobs, Random House, New York, 1984.

7. As of September 1, 1983, 79 countries had ratified the International Covenant on Economic, Social and Cultural Rights, while eight had signed but not yet ratified it. Regarding the International Covenant on Civil and Political Rights, 76 countries had ratified it while nine had signed but not yet ratified it. And regarding the Optional Protocol to the International Covenant on Civil and Political Rights, only 30 countries have ratified it and only nine have signed it. Canada has ratified all three covenants and recognized the competence of the Human Rights Committee under article 41 of the International Covenant on Civil and Political Rights. The U.S. has signed only the first two and they are not yet ratified. See *Human Rights: International Instruments, Signatures, Ratifications, Accessions, etc.*, United Nations, Geneva, September 1, 1983.

8. Article 1, Part 1 of the International Covenant on Economic and Social and Cultural Rights, of *The International Bill of Human Rights*, United Nations, New York, 1978.

9. One proposal to establish human rights criteria for the allocation of such general funds was made by the Canadian Taskforce on the Churches and Corporate Responsibility to the Canadian Minister of Finance in 1983. Specifically, it recommended that an amendment be made to the Canadian Bretton Woods Agreement Act and incorporate, "that Canada oppose an application to the International Monetary Fund (IMF) from any government that is engaged

in or that condones consistent and gross violations of basic human rights, for drawing and standby credits in excess of its gold tranche." And to serve as a "minimum definition of basic violations of human rights," TCCR identified five violations: arbitrary deprivation of life; arbitrary arrest, detention, or exile; torture or cruel, inhuman or degrading treatment or punishment; denial of the right to leave any country, including one's own, and to return to one's country; the practice of apartheid.

They also pointed out that their definition referred not to isolated instances of human rights but to a "pattern of human rights infractions that are systematic and consistent and that have been in existence over a prolonged period of time." See *Proposal to Establish Basic Human Rights Criteria as a Co-Determinant of Canada's Voting Decisions in the International Monetary Fund (IMF)*, prepared by The Taskforce on the Churches and Corporate Responsibility, Toronto, 1983.

Another proposal was put forward as a Private Member Bill by David MacDonald, M.P., to the Canadian House of Commons during the 2nd session, 30th Parliament, 1976-77. Known as Bill C-404, "An Act to prohibit aid to foreign countries violating human rights," it proposed that countries that engage in or condone a consistent pattern of gross violations of the United Nations' *Universal Declaration of Human Rights*, including any cruel, inhuman or degrading treatment or punishment, any prolonged detention without charge or any other flagrant denial of the right to life, liberty and the security of person, not receive aid or other official credit from Canada. This bill was defeated. See *The House of Commons of Canada, Private Member Bill C-404*, put forward by David MacDonald, M.P. (Egmont). An act to prohibit aid to foreign countries violating human rights, First Reading, March 3, 1977.

10. While a recipient country should select the project for which it is trying to secure aid funding, the donor country need not fund any project it feels is not for humanitarian ends. For example, we doubt that taxpayers in any country would want their aid dollars to fund military projects, or extravagant expenditures such as anniversary celebrations for a leader or a country.

11. *Perpetuating Poverty: The Political Economy of Canadian*

*Foreign Aid* by Robert Carty and Virginia Smith, Between the Lines Publishers, 1981, Toronto.

12. A "tax deduction" is used to reduce taxable income, and helps a taxpayer in proportion to his income. Someone in a 25 percent tax bracket who gives a $100 donation, for example, would have his taxes reduced by $25, while a more affluent taxpayer in a 50 percent tax bracket would save $50 in taxes. A "tax credit", on the other hand, is not related to a taxpayer's income, only to the size of his donation. If a 50 percent tax credit were given, then all taxpayers would benefit by the same $50 on a $100 donation.

# Appendix

## *Citizens' Groups and Other Sources*

ARC, Anthropology Resource Center, a Washington-based public interest group which researches issues of human rights, indigenous peoples and natural resource development

The Anti-Slavery Society, a London-based charity which is the world's oldest human rights organization and is funded by an international membership, donations and grants from charitable foundations

ASTRA, Application of Science and Technology to Rural Areas, a Bangalore-based research group which stresses understanding of local needs in the development of appropriate technology, and is affiliated with the Indian Institute of Science

CCNR, Canadian Coalition for Nuclear Responsibility, a Montreal-based non profit organization which promotes responsible decision making in the nuclear industry

nal, research and service organization which protects the interests of consumers and the environment

Comite Francais de Defense des Droits de l'Homme en Haiti, a Lyon-based non-governmental organization which supports the efforts of Haitain citizens to influence development in their own country

Earthscan, a international information service on development and environmental issues, operated by the IIED and financially supported by UNEP, the World Bank and several Western governments

ELC, Environment Liaison Centre, a Nairobi-based non government organizaton which provides a link with the U.N. Environment Program, helps an international network of over 200 member groups work on issues of environment and development, and is supported by grants from UNEP, various Western governments, foundations and membership fees

EPI, Environmental Policy Institute, a Washington-based public interest group working in the fields of energy and water resources

FOE, Friends of the Earth, an international network of private voluntary organizatons, each of which works on environmental issues in its own region

Gandhi Peace Foundation, a New Delhi-based organization which provides information, support and training to groups working in non-violent ways towards development and peace with justice

IIM, Indian Institute of Management, a Bangalore-based group researching science, technology transfer and development

Indonesian Environmental Forum, a Jakarta-based network of private voluntary organizations active in the fields of environment and development, and supported by corporations, foundations and government

IIED, International Institute for Environment and Development, a London-based research organization that concentrates on environmental issues and is primarily funded by corporations, international aid agencies and foundations

IOCU, International Organization of Consumers' Unions, a Penang-based network of consumers' associations which promotes world wide cooperation in consumer protection, information and education

IPSEP, International Project for Soft Energy Paths, a San Francisco based project of Friends of the Earth, which researches and distributes information on soft energy technology and policy

ITDG, International Technology Development Group, a London-based non government organization which develops alternative technologies and publishes and distributes information about them

IUCN, the International Union for Conservation of Nature and Natural Resources, a Geneva-based conservation network which promotes the protection and sustainable use of living resources, and is supported by the World Wildlife Fund

IWGIA, International Work Group for Indigenous Affairs, an independent Copenhagen-based research organization which provides information on the oppression of indigenous peoples and raises funds through publication sales

KENGO, Kenya Energy Non-governmental Organizations Association, a Nairobi-based coalition of groups working on renewable energy and community development in Kenya, funded by foundations, corporations, government and the United Nations

LAWG, Latin America Working Group, a Toronto-based independent non-profit research institute which works to create a broader understanding of Latin America within the Canadian community, and is funded by institutions and individual donations

Lokoyan, an Indian network which promotes democratic and decentralized development for India and is supported by personal donations and contributed labour

NRDC, National Resources Defense Council, a Washington-based lobby group which works to preserve the global environment and is funded by individual contributions

Nautilus Inc., a California-based public-interest group which researches the interrelationship of energy, environment and development, and the effects of U.S. policies on developing countries

NSI, North South Institute, an Ottawa-based non-profit corporation providing professional, policy-relevant research on North-South issues of relations between industrialized and developing countries, and funded by foundations and government

ODC, Overseas Development Council, a Washington-based non profit organization established to increase American understanding of developing countries and funded by foundations, corporations and private individuals

PAN, Pesticide Action Network, a Penang-based international network which publicizes information about global pesticide use and promotes safer methods of pest control

REECA, Renewable Energy and Environmental Conservation Association in Developing Countries, an organization with head offices in Nairobi, Lahore and Guatemala City which provides information and support for a network of environmental groups in Asia, Africa and Latin America

RFF, Resources for the Future, a Washington-based research organization focussing on the development, conservation and use of natural resources and supported by foundations, U.S. government agencies and private industry

SAM, Sahabat Alam Malaysia (Friends of the Earth Malaysia),

a Penang-based, private, non-profit citizens' action group that concentrates on issues related to the environment in Malaysia

SID, Society for International Development, a Rome-based non government organization which encourages international dialogue on major development issues

Survival International, a London-based international charity working to help tribal peoples to exercise their right to survival and self-determination

TCCR, Taskforce on Churches and Corporate Responsibility, a Toronto-based national ecumenical coalition established to ask questions of corporate and social responsibility in the area of human rights and social justice, and funded exclusively by the member churches

WCC, World Council of Churches, a Geneva-based ecumenical body sponsoring research on theological and social issues, with members from over 300 Orthodox and Western churches

WISE, World Information Service on Energy, an Amsterdam-based international network of safe energy groups which distributes information on energy and is funded by sales of publications
WRI, World Resources Institute, a Washington-based non profit research center that concentrates on resource policy options and is supported by foundations

Worldwatch Institute, a Washington-based non profit research organization which analyzes and focusses attention on global problems, and is funded by private foundations and U.N. organizations

*National and International Organizations*

AfDB, African Development Bank, an Abidjan-based multilateral bank with large voting shares held by Nigeria, Libya, Algeria, Zaire, Canada and France

AID, United States Agency for International Development, the United States' official bilateral aid agency, based in Washington

BADEA, Arab Bank for Economic Development in Africa, a Khartoum based bank which provides funding and technical assistance for projects in Africa and whose subscribers include most members of the Arab League

ADB, Asian Development Bank, a Manila-based multilateral development bank which operates in the Asian and Pacific region and has major voting shares held by the United States, Japan, India, Australia and Canada

CIDA, Canadian International Development Agency, Canada's official bilateral aid agency, based in Ottawa

CDB, Caribbean Development Bank, a Barbados-based regional bank which provides loans and technical assistance to member countries, with major voting shares held by Jamaica, Trinidad and Tobago, Canada and the United Kingdom

FAO, Food and Agriculture Organization, a Rome-based U.N. agency which works in the areas of agriculture, nutrition and rural life

IDB, Inter-American Development Bank, a Washington-based multilateral bank which provides loans to South and Central American countries, and whose voting power is largely controlled by the United States, Argentina and Brazil, Mexico, Venezuela and Canada

IBRD, (World Bank) International Bank for Reconstruction and Development, a Washington-based multilateral bank which provides loans to governments of member nations, with major voting shares held by the United States, Germany, Japan, the United Kingdom France and Canada

IDRC, International Development Research Centre, an Ottawa-based crown corporation which supports research designed to adapt science and technology to the needs of developing countries, and is financed by the Parliament of Canada

ILO, International Labour Organization, a Geneva-based U.N. agency concentrating on labor conditions, living standards and social justice issues

ODA, Overseas Development Administration, Britain's official bil ateral aid agency based in London

OECD, Organization for Economic Cooperation and Development, a Paris-based organization which promotes policies contributing to sustainable economic growth and the expansion of world trade, and is funded by member nations, including Canada, the United States, Australia and most European countries

SIDA, Swedish International Development Agency, Sweden's official bilateral aid agency, based in Stockholm

UNCTAD, United Nations Conference on Trade and Development, a Geneva-based U.N. organization which promotes international trade and economic development

UNDP, United Nations Development Programme, a New York-based U.N. agency which provides developing countries with technical and preinvestment assistance

UNESCO, United Nations Educational, Scientific and Cultural Organization, a Paris-based U.N. agency which encourages international dialogue on culture, science and education

UNEP, United Nations Environment Programme, a Nairobi-based UN agency which serves as a liaison body for non governmental organizations, governments and the U.N. on environmental issues

UNICEF, United Nations International Childrens Fund, a U.N. agency which assists children throughout the world, particularly in developing countries

# Index

# About Probe International

In Canada, Probe International works to reform agencies such as the federal government's Canadian International Development Agency and the Canadian Export Development Corporation, which both believe people in the Third World aren't entitled to the same environmental standards as Canadians. We also work to reform international agencies that are funded with Canadian tax dollars, such as the World Bank and other international financial institutions. We believe that people in the Third World, like people everywhere, should have full rights to a say in development projects that affect their lives, and we especially object to foisting on them pesticides, drugs, and technologies that are banned in the affluent countries.

In the Third World, we work closely with grass roots organizations that are fighting to protect their environment. We strengthen their hand by publicizing their information worldwide, and by searching out and obtaining for them corporate and aid agency documents that are being kept secret. Likewise, they strengthen our hand with detailed information about how our corporations and aid agencies wreak havoc, helping to stop destructive projects and to make our institutions accountable.

In a democracy, there is no greater guarantee of justice than the free flow of information. Probe International names names. Because we aren't dependent on governments or industry for our funding, we are free to reveal exactly who is doing what, and when. Probe International is an independent environmental advocacy organization, accountable only to the public at large. The bulk of our funding comes in the form of small donations from the general public.

Probe International
225 Brunswick Avenue
Toronto, Ontario
Canada M5S 2M6